cookies

This edition published in 2011 by
CHARTWELL BOOKS, INC.
A division of BOOK SALES, INC.
276 Fifth Avenue Suite 206
New York, New York 10001
USA

This edition published by arrangement with Flame Tree Publishing,
an imprint of The Foundry Creative Media Company Limited
Crabtree Hall, Crabtree Lane
Fulham, London SW6 6TY
United Kingdom
www.flametreepublishing.com

Publisher's Note:
Raw or semicooked eggs should not be consumed by babies, toddlers, pregnant or breast-feeding women,
the elderly, or people with a chronic illness.

Publisher & Creative Director: Nick Wells
Senior Project Editor: Catherine Taylor
Introductory text: Gina Steer
Art Director: Mike Spender
Layout Design: Jane Ashley
Digital Design & Production: Chris Herbert
Proofreader: Dawn Laker

Special thanks to Laura Bulbeck, Digby Smith and Helen Wall.

ISBN-13: 978-0-7858-2863-1

Printed in China

All images © Foundry Arts except the following, which are courtesy of Shutterstock and © the following photographers: Bragin Alexey 10r; mayer kleinostheim
11r; Elzbieta Sekowska 13bl; Lori Sparkia 13br; IngridHS 14r; nastiakru 14l; Tanis Saucier 15tl; tarasov 15bl; marilyn barbone 16l; jsimagedesign 18r; Shebeko 18l;
David Stuart, Photographer 19br; Marie C Fields 20; Poulsons Photography 21; Cindy Haggerty 22tr; wavebreakmedia ltd 24; Elena Elisseeva 30tl; Courtesy of
and © Foundry Arts41; matka_Wariatka 42tl; Payless Images 43; Tereza Dvorak 44; bonchan 46; Evgeniya Uvarova 47; Monkey Business Images 31, 37br.

cookies

Gina Steer

CHARTWELL
BOOKS, INC.

Contents

Introduction

Where did it all start, this love affair with cookies? Well, rumor has it that back in the twelfth century, Richard the Lionheart of England took "ship's biscuits" on his ships in order to feed the crew throughout the long and arduous voyages across the oceans to fight the Arabs in the name of Christianity. These biscuits certainly would not appeal to today's consumers because they were made from barley, rye, and bean flours and wrapped in cheesecloth. However, by the time that the Armada set sail in 1588, hard and long-lasting "ship's biscuits" had become a normal addition to the seaman's fayre and they were allocated a daily allowance of 1 pound per person.

It was the British writer Samuel Pepys who put biscuits firmly on the menu. He was commissioned to work out the daily allowance of food and drink for all seamen, and he decreed that this allowance should include 1 pound of wheaten biscuits that were clean and sound (without the weevils, which had inhabited biscuits in the past). He also included for all a daily allowance of a gallon of beer, which, as can be imagined, was most popular with all.

Biscuits played an important part in Admiral Nelson's fleets, helping to sustain the sailors before, during, and after the many battles and expeditions that were undertaken by the British navy commander. This daily allowance continued for all seamen until the introduction of bread in the middle of the nineteenth century. Nowadays, "ship's biscuits" can still be found in the galleys of yachts and other small boats. Also relying heavily on biscuits for sustenance were the men who braved the elements to conquer the North and South Poles.

Evolution

So how did ship's biscuits lead to the sweet cookies we know and love today? Well, while seamen were eating their "biscuits," which arguably evolved into the more savory or simple end of the spectrum, such as crackers and plain cookies, bakers around the world began employing the techniques they had developed for cakes—the use of butter,

eggs, and sugar to enrich and lighten—to create sweeter, more luxurious "biscuits"—or, as we know them, "cookies". And, as the supply of sugar and the refinement of flour improved, so such products became more easily produced and widely available—all with their own distinct styles according to the flavorings and ingredients typical of the country.

It was in the eighteenth century that cookies started to be made commercially. Gradually they began to appear in grocery stores, and so began the great love affair.

What's in a Name?

So, "cookie" or "biscuit"? If you live in the United States, all flat, crisp or chewy, sweet treats are called "cookies"—which is from the Dutch *koekje*, meaning "small cake"—and a "biscuit" is a small, soft leavened bread. However, in Britain, the sweet treats are called both "biscuits" and "cookies," the latter often being reserved for the big chunky kind with chocolate chips. Whatever you call them, cookies are enjoyed by many as a midmorning snack with coffee or to accompany a cup of iced or hot tea.

The Joy of Making Your Own

Homemade cookies are quick and easy to make, do not require many ingredients, and are delicious afternoon snacks, often giving a much-needed energy boost for any time on any occasion. There are many variations that can be made, with many types of cookie dough. Once you start baking, you will be able to vary the recipes according to your own personal preference, providing irresistible treats for the whole family. Another advantage of making your own cookies is that you can control which ingredients you use, thus ensuring that none of the ingredients will trigger any allergies and that you know what you are eating.

In this book, you will quickly discover how easy it is to make and bake cookies, and you will find many different varieties for you to try. Once you have mastered the basic principles, you will discover for yourself a host of the most mouthwatering delights.

About This Book

Before you dive into the main section of recipes, there is plenty of invaluable information in this book. First, the many different categories of cookie are explained, including more speciality varieties, such as rolled cookies and drop cookies, each with a basic recipe, and some invaluable hints. Then we delve into how to achieve a perfect result every time, offering the reader ideas concerning the correct equipment to use, from which paper to choose to the tools for removing the cooked cookies from the baking sheets, plus information regarding the oven. All of this will make baking far easier, and there are also some invaluable storage ideas.

A comprehensive list of ingredients is provided, ranging from dried fruits and how to use them in baking, to the correct fat, sugar, and flour to use. All have storage instructions, to ensure that all the ingredients stay fresh for as long as possible. We then discuss the decoration of cookies, explaining how they can easily be embellished before baking, or after, once cool. Finally, before our main selection of recipes, some delicious recipes for cookies from around the world are provided—choose from these suggestions, including Anzac Cookies, Langues de Chat, and Swedish Gingerbread.

So how to get started? Have a good look through the book, then pick a recipe. Make sure you first read the recipe to the end to check you have all the ingredients and equipment and to make sure you understand the method and timing, then assemble and measure the ingredients. Do not forget to turn the oven on, to give it time to reach the correct temperature.

Happy baking!

Equipment and Utensils

Baking Sheets

I prefer a nonstick baking sheet—also called a cookie sheet—that has either lower sides than a baking pan or

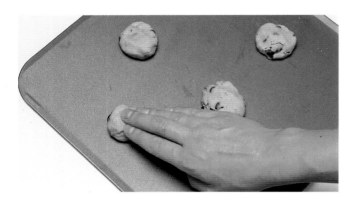

only one side for gripping. This is because, without the higher sides of a pan, the heat penetrates the uncooked dough more quickly, producing a more uniform color and texture. If the sheet is lightly oiled, then the cooked cookies, with the aid of a spatula, can be gently pushed onto a wire cooling rack without risk of them breaking.

Papers

There are some cookies that are better if the sheet is first lined. There are several different lining papers that can be used.

Wax Paper

An invaluable aid in the kitchen, wax paper has been around for many years. Wax paper is made moisture-proof by the application of wax. Because the wax can melt at high

temperatures and affect the flavor of baked items, it should not be used for lining baking sheets when baking cookies.

However, it is suitable for lining cake pans to bake cakes, and wax paper can be used to wrap cooked cookies once they cool down, because it will keep the moisture out so that they retain their crisp texture. It is readily available in grocery stores.

Nonstick Parchment Paper

Nonstick parchment paper is now used extensively in baking and often replaces wax paper. There is often no need to oil when lining pans; however, a little oil is useful, because it helps to keep the paper together and in one place before the mixture is put into the pan.

Reusable Silicone-Treated Parchment Paper

This paper can be used time and time again because it is washable. It is available in a roll or already cut; simply place a sheet on the baking sheet. There are also precut pieces that fit the bottom and sides of cake pans. It can also be used to wrap food that will be cooked in the oven or the microwave, as well as for storing food in the refrigerator and freezer. Look for it in specialty baking shops and online.

Rice Paper

This is not used so much these days, mainly being reserved for making macaroons or petit fours. As its name implies, it is made from rice and has a translucent appearance. It is edible, with a soft papery texture and is used when it could be difficult to remove a lining paper from the product.

Other Essential Items

Measuring Cups

These come in sets, using ¼, ⅓, ½, and 1 cup, for measuring dry ingredients. Make sure you level off the ingredient unless otherwise instructed. Keep the markings on a liquid measuring cup at eye level to measure the correct amount. Baking needs 100 per-cent accuracy to ensure a perfect result. It is not something that can be guessed—too much flour, for example, can make a mixture heavy and inedible.

Standard Measuring Spoons

Essential for all baking, because they will provide accurate measurements of ingredients—especially essential when measuring strong flavors, such as spices, and for leavening agents, such as baking powder, cream of tartar, and baking soda. Too much leavening agent will result in the mixture rising far too quickly, then collapsing.

Sifters and Strainers

Sifters are used for sifting flour and confectioners' sugar to incorporate air and remove lumps, as well as for dusting finished foods with confectioners' sugar or unsweetened cocoa. Strainers, either metal or nylon, are useful for separating solids from liquids, and fine-mesh ones can also be used for sifting.

Mixing Bowls

Assorted sizes are a good investment. The larger bowls can be used for making cookies, while the smaller ones are ideal for melting ingredients, such as chocolate (with this in mind, make sure you choose heatproof bowls such as Pyrex), as well as for mixing icings and frostings.

Spatulas

A spatula with a long handle and slim blade about 1 inch wide is perfect for removing the cooked items from the baking sheet, as well as for spreading frosting or icing. Plastic spatulas are useful for folding flour or whisked egg white into a creamed mixture of butter and sugar, and for scraping all the uncooked mixture out of a mixing bowl to avoid wasting any. A broad, flat spatula with slits is an equally useful tool for removing the cooked cookies from the baking sheet.

Rolling Pin

An essential tool for rolling out the dough prior to cutting and baking.

Cutters

There are many different cutters available in metal or plastic, all suitable for cutting out the uncooked dough. If you have small children, look for animal cutters, or perhaps letters so you can make cookies that form a name. There are also plain and fluted, round or square cutters in different sizes, as well as heart-shape cutters—not to mention gingerbread people, holly leaves, and Christmas bells.

When using, make sure that the dough is of an even thickness and you put the cutter squarely on the rolled dough for a uniform and even result. When washing the dishes, make sure that the cutter is thoroughly clean and completely dry—especially in the case of metal cutters, so that they do not go rusty. Store in a dry place. An excellent idea is to tie together cutters that are the same shape in varying sizes.

Wire Cooling Rack

An invaluable tool for all baking. Coming either as an oblong or round, with small feet so it stands above the countertop, it enables cooked cookies to cool before being iced or stored. It is imperative that all baked items are cooled completely before storing, otherwise they will become soggy.

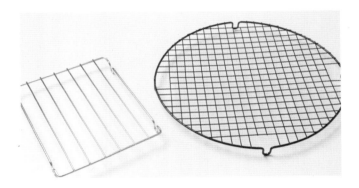

Pastry Bags and Tips

The best pastry bags to use are nylon bags that can be placed in the washing machine to ensure they are completely clean after use. Once dry, store in a clean bag or small box. An assortment of tips is another good investment. Choose thin writing tips as well as small and medium star tips.

Ingredients

There are three main ingredients when making cookies: fat, flour, and sugar. However, it is all the other ingredients used that make the many different varieties. Below is a comprehensive list of these ingredients, with hints and tips on how to get the best possible results from them.

Fat

The fat element in cookies can be butter, margarine, and, in a few cases, vegetable shortening. All fats should be stored in the refrigerator and all have a shelf life, so be careful not to use out-of-date products.

Butter

Nowadays, particularly with the emphasis on cutting down the intake of salt in the diet, when using butter it is best to use unsalted butter, unless the recipe states otherwise. Be sure that it is at room temperature ("softened") so that it combines easily with the other ingredients. If it is too hard, the butter will not blend properly and there will be small globules of fat left in after baking. If the butter is too soft, it will become oily, making the cookies oily, which does not taste good.

Margarine

If using margarine, use hard block margarine, not the soft margarine in containers, because these do not withstand high heat and will break down when heated to a high temperature. When using margarine, it results in a more bland taste.

Vegetable Shortening

This again produces a blander flavor than butter. It also produces a different texture—it will be very crumbly. Many years ago lard might have been used in these instances, but these days it is seldom used due to heart and other health concerns.

Sugar

Sugar is normally used for the sweetness in cookies, instead of honey or corn syrup, because the consistency of honey and syrup is too thin and would not provide a firm enough dough.

Granulated Sugars

The best sugar to use is superfine sugar, because the smaller grains melt more easily, but regular granulated sugar can also be used. If you don't have superfine sugar, you can make some by processing the same amount of regular sugar in a food processor for about a minute. If unbleached sugars are used, you can reduce the amount slightly because they are a little sweeter. Turbinado (raw) sugar or light brown sugar can also be used.

Confectioners' Sugar

Also known as powdered sugar, confectioners' sugar is used in two ways when making cookies. It can be used in the actual dough to give a smooth texture to the finished cookies, such as in Viennese Whirls, but also to decorate the cookies before serving. The two most commonly made toppings for cookies are icing or buttercream (*see* page 38).

Storing and Using Sugar

Once sugar has been opened, it is a good idea to keep it in storage containers. Always use up the sugar in the containers before opening a fresh package. If storing confectioners' sugar

in its package, make sure that it is closed properly, otherwise moisture and air will get to the sugar, which will quickly harden and form lumps that can be difficult to remove. Sift confectioners' sugar before using, otherwise the icing will be full of lumps and will not coat adequately.

Flour

Which to Use

All-purpose white flour is the flour most commonly used, but self-rising flour is available. If you don't have any self-rising, you can substitute 1 cup all-purpose flour plus 1½ teaspoons baking powder and ½ teaspoon salt per 1 cup of

self-rising flour. In the "healthier" types of cookies, whole-wheat flour can be used, but be careful not to use too much of the bran husks because it will alter the texture of the dough.

Storing

Once opened, flour keeps best if poured into storage containers and kept in a cool place. Rotate the flour occasionally and check the expiration date before using. Flour stored incorrectly and for too long can become infested with insects. If this happens, discard immediately and thoroughly wash and disinfect the area where the flour was kept. Also check other ingredients that were stored with the flour.

Spices, Seeds and Other Tasty Additions

Spices play an important part in cooking, and never more so than in baking. It is a way of imparting great flavors, which can make the difference between a boring and tasteless cookie and an explosion of flavor. Spices that are suitable to be used include ground cinnamon, apple pie spice, ground cloves, ground allspice, ground ginger, saffron, cardamom seeds, caraway seeds, and poppy seeds. Sesame seeds are also a good addition and can be toasted or left plain before use.

Spice Advice

When buying spices and seeds, it is important to buy only in small quantities, because they quickly lose their pungency—especially the ground spices. Where they are stored also plays an important role in retaining their taste and aroma. Keep in a cool, dark place and not in a spice rack on display in the kitchen. They may look good displayed like this, but they will not taste good and there would be little point using them. Measure carefully with measuring spoons; too much can be overpowering, not enough will result in cookies that are bland and uninteresting.

Dried Lavender

This is a lesser thought of but delightful ingredient for cookies. Hang bunches upside down in a warm, dry place and, once dry, carefully remove the flower seeds from the dried plant and use. Lavender has a strong flavor, so use sparingly. Store in airtight containers in a cool, dark place.

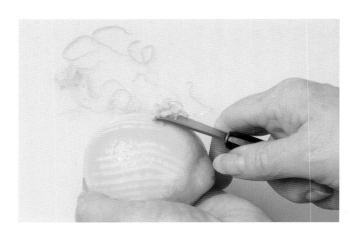

Zests

Finely grated citrus zest can be used to add zing to cookies. Orange, lemon, and lime are the best and, if possible, choose organic fruits. These have not been sprayed with pesticide, nor do they have a protective wax coating, which is often applied after picking to prolong their shelf life. If you cannot find organic, scrub the zest of the fruits to be used thoroughly and let dry before using. To grate zest, use the fine holes on the grater and brush down after grating with a pastry brush to remove as much zest as possible from the grater. Store fruits in the vegetable drawer of the refrigerator, and grate as required—if grated too early, the zest will lose its flavor and become dry. The juice may also be used—squeeze after grating.

Vanilla and Almond Extracts

The two main extracts that are used in baking cookies are vanilla extract and almond extract. These have an intense flavor and should be used sparingly. Look for extracts instead of "flavorings," which are synthetic, made mainly from chemicals in laboratories instead of from the plant itself.

Rose Water and Orange Flower Water

These are extracts made from rose petals and orange blossom, and both have a very subtle and delicate flavor and aroma. They are better suited to more delicate cookies, such as petit fours.

Peppermint Extract

In baking, peppermint extract is mainly used for making Peppermint Creams, but can be used to flavor cakes and cookies. It has a powerful flavor and should be used sparingly. A few drops is all that is normally required. Peppermint extract is a herb extract. However, there are also synthetic substitutes available, so look carefully at the label when buying.

With all extracts, it is best to keep them in a cool, dark place and, once opened, to use as quickly as possible. Make sure that the lid is screwed down as tightly as possible after opening.

Unsweetened Cocoa

If you want to have a chocolate flavor, in many cases unsweetened cocoa is a better option than solid chocolate. It is far easier to use because it does not need melting or grating, but simply sifting. When deciding to use unsweetened cocoa, simply substitute 1–2 tablespoons of the flour that is used in the recipe with unsweetened cocoa. Make sure it is thoroughly incorporated into the dough before rolling out, otherwise the finished result will be streaky.

Chocolate

There are many types of chocolate readily available, some specifically for cooking. This is high-quality dark chocolate and it has a high cocoa solids content (normally 70 percent), which gives an intense chocolate flavor. I would recommend that high-quality dark chocolate is grated instead of melted and stirred into the mixture. However, it would be fine melted and used to ice the tops of the cooked cookies.

Another alternative would be to use chocolate chips for baking. These come in small packages and are available in white, milk, or dark chocolate. They are not made from the best chocolate, but work well in cooking and will not melt as ordinary chocolate that has been chopped will. The finished cookie still acquires a good chocolate flavor, but will have small pieces of chocolate throughout because the chips retain their shape. Once chocolate is opened, including the chocolate chips, it needs to be used quickly. Chocolate exposed for a while to the air will bloom and the flavor will be impaired.

Coffee

Coffee is a good flavoring to use in baking, especially if combined with chopped pecans or walnuts. Use either strong coffee such as espresso or, if using instant coffee, make about 2–3 times the strength normally drunk. Do not use much;

1–2 teaspoons should be enough for ½ cup of mixture. You may need to add a little more flour if the mixture is wet sticky and difficult to roll out.

Dried Fruits

There is a wide range of dried fruits available for home baking, which offer the opportunity to bake a host of delicious cookies that will satisfy everyone's taste buds. They include sour cherries, cranberries, blueberries, mango, dried plums, dates, apricots, figs, and mixed peel, as well as currants, raisins, and golden raisins. There are also candied fruits, such as cherries, pineapple and papaya, as well as preserved ginger, plus angelica.

Using
The larger fruits need to be chopped into much smaller pieces, otherwise they will not combine well with the other ingredients. With candied fruits, such as cherries, pineapple, angelica, and dates, it is a good idea to wash them in cold or lukewarm water after chopping to remove any sticky syrup, then toss in flour to stop the chopped fruit from clumping

together. This also applies to preserved ginger. Currants, raisins, and golden raisins can be used as they are, as can sour cherries, cranberries, and blueberries.

Buy these fruits in small quantities; do not be tempted to buy in bulk unless you know that you will use them quickly. They do not have an indefinite shelf life and will quickly shrivel and start to become crystallized. Once opened, keep preferably in glass or stone containers and use within 2 months of opening. If liked, store in the refrigerator—this will extend their shelf life for up to 1 year, although it is better to use more quickly than that.

Nuts

Nutty cookies are delicious and, if not already so, will quickly become a firm favorite with both family and friends. There are many nuts to choose from, and the only rule to remember when using nuts is that they must be chopped finely so that they remain well distributed instead of sinking to the bottom of the mixture. When using nuts, it is easy to substitute a different nut to the one specified in the recipe; this will only change the finished taste, not the texture of the cooked cookies. Nuts to use include walnuts, pecans, slivered almonds, hazelnuts, macadamia nuts, and pine nuts. Once opened, store in airtight containers in a cool place. Use within a couple of weeks of opening.

Baking Perfect Cookies

Cookies are extremely easy to prepare and bake, and, providing that a few guidelines are followed, perfect results can be achieved every time. They are ideal to make when encouraging young children to cook—there is nothing better for them than to get their hands into the dough while making the cookies, cutting them out, and finally decorating the finished cookie. What joy, and good enough to encourage most children to try cooking. A great start on their culinary journey through life.

Baking Rules

- First of all, it is important that all the ingredients are assembled before starting to bake.

- Measure out the ingredients carefully—do not attempt to guess, because this will lead to poor results and the cookies could even be inedible.

- Turn the oven on at least 10 minutes before baking for it to reach the correct temperature. An oven thermometer is an excellent investment, as is a timer.

- If using a convection oven, remember to check the manufacturer's directions regarding oven temperature. In general, reduce the temperature given in a recipe by 25°F if using a convection oven.

- Use flat baking sheets that have only one raised side. High

sides all around will prevent the cookies from browning evenly. It also helps to make the baked cookies easier to remove once cooked.

- If using one baking sheet, place it in the center of the oven once the oven has been preheated and reached its correct temperature. If using two, place the oven racks so that there is the same amount of space between them. If necessary, switch the sheets around during baking so that an even browning is achieved.

- Have the ingredients at room temperature and, once the dough is made, depending on how soft it is, wrap and chill for 30 minutes, or until firm.

- Do not use excessive flour when rolling out cookies. This will destroy the balance of ingredients and end with a poor result that can be tough and heavy to eat.

- Let cooked cookies cool for a few minutes before attempting to remove them from the baking sheet, otherwise they could easily break up. Then use a large spatula to transfer them to a wire cooling rack. Once on the cooling rack, press the tops down lightly with the back of the spatula to flatten.

- With cookies made with corn syrup, let cool for 1–2 minutes, but no longer, otherwise they will harden and stick to the baking sheet, and will need warming again to remove.

Storage

Once the cookies are cooked and have become cold, it is important that they are stored correctly, otherwise they will quickly become soggy and unappetizing.

- They are best stored in an airtight cake tin lined with wax paper or aluminum foil. Layer the cookies with additional sheets of wax paper or foil. If you use a plastic container instead of a metal one, there may be a chance that stored cakes and cookies will taste musty after a while and that the cookies will turn soggy.

- Store different types of cookies separately, preferably without icing.

- If plain cooked cookies become soggy, reheat them in the oven at 325°F for 5 minutes. Be careful that they do not overbrown.

Basic Recipes

Here, we provide recipes for the many types of cookies that it is possible to create, all of which are quick and easy to make and bake, as well as being totally delicious.

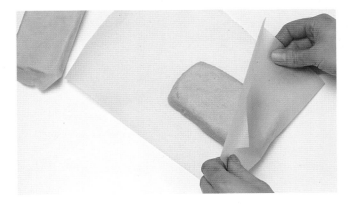

Basic Refrigerator Cookies

The dough for these cookies lends itself to being kept in the refrigerator for up to 3 weeks before being baked. It must be well wrapped while being stored in the refrigerator, and it can be sliced and baked as required.

Makes 20–24

2 tbsp. unsalted butter, softened
⅔ cup superfine sugar
1 large egg yolk
1 tsp. vanilla extract
2⅓ cups plus 1 tbsp. all-purpose flour

Preheat the oven to 350°F. Beat the butter and sugar together until blended, then stir in the egg yolk with the vanilla extract. Add the flour and, using your hands, bring the mixture together until a soft dough is formed.

Knead until smooth and pliable, then form into a roll. Wrap in parchment paper and chill in the refrigerator for at least 30 minutes.

When ready to cook, lightly oil two baking sheets and slice the dough into rounds. Place on the baking sheets. Cook in the preheated oven for 15–20 minutes until golden brown. Remove from the oven and let cool for 2–3 minutes before transferring to a wire rack. Let stand until cold before decorating.

Helpful Hint These cookies can be flavored with ground ginger, cinnamon, allspice, or grated lemon or orange zest—use in place of the vanilla extract. If liked, decorate the top with an icing, buttercream, melted chocolate, or even fresh cream. If storing in the refrigerator for longer than a few hours, wrap in both parchment paper and aluminum foil.

Piped Cookies

These look very impressive and are really simple to make, so they are perfect when catering for large numbers.

Viennese Whirls

There are many different recipes for these delicious cookies. The basic recipe is flavored with vanilla extract, but it could be replaced with finely grated citrus zest or even rose water or orange flower water.

Makes 20–24

1 cup (2 sticks) unsalted butter, softened
⅔ cup confectioners' sugar, sifted
1 tsp. vanilla extract
2 cups all-purpose flour, sifted
2 tsp. baking powder
1½ tbsp. cornstarch, sifted
½ tsp. salt
confectioners' sugar, to dust

Preheat the oven to 350°F about 10 minutes before baking. Lightly oil two or three baking sheets. Fit a large pastry bag with a large star tip. Cream the butter with the confectioners' sugar and vanilla extract, then gradually beat in the flour together with the baking powder, cornstarch, and salt.

Spoon about one-quarter of the mixture into the pastry bag and pipe whirls onto the oiled baking sheets. Repeat until all the mixture is used. Bake in the preheated oven for 12–15 minutes until pale golden. Remove and let cool before transferring to a wire rack. Let stand until cold before dusting with confectioners' sugar and serving.

Helpful Hint If liked, the cookies can be sandwiched together with either whipped cream or buttercream.

No-Bake Cookies

Here, the cookies normally use either light corn syrup or melted chocolate to keep the other ingredients together. Instead of baking, they "set," making them a perfect choice for kids to create. Make sure that an adult does the chopping and monitors the melting of the corn syrup or chocolate. Kids love making them because it is the perfect excuse to get messy.

Nutty Chocolate No-Bake Cookies

Makes 12–14

6 tbsp. unsalted butter
¼ cup packed light brown or turbinado (raw) sugar
2 oz. semisweet dark chocolate, broken into squares
½ cup mixed nuts or dried fruit, or a mixture of both, chopped
½ –⅔ cup crushed Graham crackers

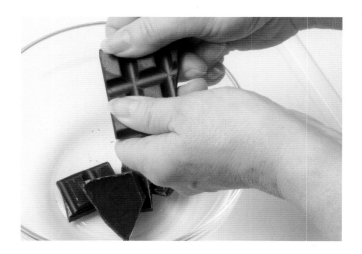

Place the butter, sugar, and chocolate in a heavy saucepan and place over gentle heat. Heat gently, stirring occasionally with a wooden spoon, until smooth and blended.

Remove from the heat and stir in the nuts and/or fruit and enough crushed Graham crackers to make a firm mixture. Stir until well blended.

Line two baking sheets with nonstick parchment paper. Place small spoonfuls of the dough on the lined baking sheets. Let set in the refrigerator for at least 2 hours before serving. Store covered in the refrigerator.

Helpful Hint When serving these cookies, be careful that they are not given to anyone who has a nut allergy. The nuts in this recipe can easily be replaced with dried fruits or chocolate chips.

Drop Cookies

Drop cookies are made from a dough that is soft enough to be dropped or spooned straight onto the baking sheet but that is still stiff enough to need slightly flattening down. If too soft, it will run off the baking sheet during baking.

Double Chocolate Cookies

These drop cookies are quick and easy to make and are really popular with both family and friends.

Makes 20–24

6 tbsp. unsalted butter, softened
⅓ cup granulated sugar
⅓ cup packed light brown sugar
1 tsp. vanilla extract
1 large egg, beaten
1¼ cups self-rising flour
¼ cup unsweetened cocoa, sifted
¼ cup chocolate chips

Preheat the oven to 350°F about 10 minutes before baking. Lightly oil two baking sheets and set aside. Beat the butter with the granulated sugar and brown sugar until combined, then stir in the vanilla extract.

Slowly beat in the egg, adding a little flour after each addition. When all the egg has been added, stir in the remaining flour together with the unsweetened cocoa and chocolate chips.

Drop spoonfuls onto the prepared baking sheets and flatten slightly with the back of a spoon or your hand. Bake in the preheated oven for 12–15 minutes until firm to the touch. Remove from the oven and let cool for 1 minute before transferring to a wire rack. Let stand until cold before serving.

Helpful Hint Leave room on the baking sheets for the cookies to expand.

Shaped Cookies

These cookies are made from firm dough that is rolled out on a lightly floured surface and cut into shapes with pastry cutters. The dough is similar in consistency to flaky pastry.

Two well-known shaped cookies are shortbread and gingerbread people. The cookies can be iced, spread with melted chocolate, or left plain.

Shortbread

This classic recipe is one of the most versatile of all. It can be baked whole as a circle then cut into sections, or cut into all kinds of shapes, numbers, letters, fluted circles, squares, or triangles, all depending on which cutter is used.

Makes 18–20

1⅓ cups plus 1 tbsp. all-purpose white flour
8 tbsp. unsalted butter, softened
¼ cup superfine sugar, plus extra for sprinkling

Preheat the oven to 350°F. Place all the ingredients either in a food processor and process for 1–2 minutes until combined, or in a mixing bowl and use your fingertips to knead the ingredients together until a ball is formed in the bottom of the bowl.

Remove the dough from the processor or bowl, place on a lightly floured surface, and knead until a smooth and pliable dough is formed.

Roll out on a lightly floured surface to a thickness of ¼ inch and cut into shapes. Place on lightly oiled baking sheets and prick the tops lightly with a fork. Bake in the preheated oven for 15–20 minutes until pale golden.

Remove from the oven and let cool for 5 minutes before transferring to a wire rack. Let stand until cold before serving or decorating.

Helpful Hint Flavor can easily be introduced by adding them to the ingredients before mixing everything together. Try finely grated lemon, lime or orange zest, or 1–2 teaspoons ground ginger, ground cinnamon, or allspice. The cookies can also be made chocolate-flavored by replacing ¼ cup of the flour with ⅓ cup sifted unsweetened cocoa.

Bar Cookies

Here, the mixture is either poured or pressed normally into an oblong baking pan, baked, and cut into bars to serve. There are many different recipes for bar cookies, ranging from the really elaborate, where there are three layers, such as a pastry shell topped with a caramel topping, and iced, to simple favorites, such as the recipe on the next page.

Coconut Chocolate Chews

These can be served plain, or iced with a white or coffee icing. For extra decadence, try topping with melted chocolate.

Makes 10–20, depending on how they are cut

8 tbsp. unsalted butter, softened
¼ cup granulated sugar
1 tbsp. unsweetened cocoa, sifted
1 cup all-purpose flour, sifted
2 cups dry unsweetened flaked coconut
1⅓ cups confectioners' sugar, sifted, for the icing

Preheat the oven to 350°F about 10 minutes before baking. Lightly oil a 7-inch square baking pan. Beat the butter and sugar until creamy, then beat in the unsweetened cocoa.

Stir in the flour and then the coconut. Stir until well blended. Place in the oiled pan and press down firmly. Bake in the preheated oven for 20–25 minutes until the top feels firm when touched lightly with a clean finger. Remove from the oven and let cool.

Mix the confectioners' sugar with about 2–3 tablespoons hot water to form a smooth icing, and pour over the cooled chews. Let stand until set before cutting into bars or squares to serve. Store in an airtight container.

Helpful Hint If liked, top with a white icing, then pipe on thin lines of melted chocolate and, before the chocolate sets, drag a clean skewer through the lines to create a feathered effect.

Basic Butter-Rich Cookies

By adding various ingredients to this basic dough, you will be able to make many different variations.

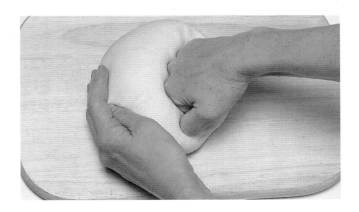

Makes 20–24

8 tbsp. unsalted butter, softened
⅔ cup superfine sugar, plus extra for sprinkling (optional)
1 large egg yolk
1 tsp. vanilla extract
1¾ cups all-purpose flour

Preheat the oven to 350°F. Cream the butter with the sugar until light and fluffy, then beat in the egg and vanilla extract. Add the flour and mix until the mixture comes together and forms a ball in the bottom of the mixing bowl.

Place the dough on a lightly floured surface or board and knead until smooth. Either shape into small rounds and

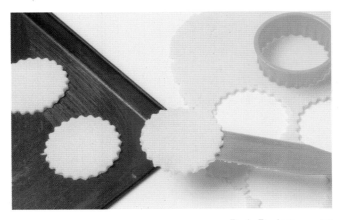

flatten with your hand, or roll out to a thickness of ¼ inch and cut into rounds or shapes.

Place on lightly buttered or oiled baking sheets, leaving room for expansion. Prick lightly with a fork and, if liked, sprinkle with a little superfine sugar. Bake in the preheated oven for 15 minutes, or until pale golden.

Remove from the oven and let cool for 2–3 minutes before transferring to wire racks. Let stand until cold before storing in airtight containers.

Helpful Hint If liked, shape the dough into a roll, wrap in parchment paper and plastic wrap, and store in the refrigerator. The dough can be left in there for up to 3 weeks. Remove the dough from the refrigerator 20–30 minutes before using.

Rolled Cookies

These are the easiest and most commonly made cookies, from which many of our favorite varieties can be made. The beauty of these is that, not only do they taste really delicious, but they are also quick and easy to make.

Fruity Rolled Cookies

By adding various ingredients, such as in this recipe, to the basic dough, you will be able to make many different varieties, both sweet and savory.

Makes 20–24

8 tbsp. unsalted butter, softened
⅔ cup superfine sugar, plus 1–2 tsp. for sprinkling
¼ cup dried currants
1 tbsp. finely grated lemon zest
1 large egg yolk
1¾ cups all-purpose flour

Preheat the oven to 350°F. Cream the butter with the sugar until light and fluffy, then stir in the currants and lemon zest. Add the egg yolk, then the flour. Mix together either in a food mixer or with your hand to form a smooth dough.

Place on a lightly floured surface or board and knead until smooth. Roll out to a thickness of ¼ inch and, using a 2-inch fluted cutter, cut into circles. Place on lightly buttered or oiled baking sheets, leaving a little room for expansion. Prick lightly with a fork and sprinkle with a little superfine sugar. Bake in the preheated oven for 12–15 minutes until pale golden.

Remove from the oven and let cool for 5 minutes before transferring to a wire rack. Let stand until cold before storing in airtight containers.

Helpful Hint Other ingredients that can be used include finely chopped preserved ginger, chopped candied cherries, dried cranberries, chocolate chips, ground cinnamon, and allspice. Use in place of the dried currants and zest. For savory cookies, replace the sugar with 1 cup finely grated strong cheese, such as Parmesan or cheddar, and replace the currants and lemon zest with 1 tsp. dry mustard powder. Dried herbs can also be added, as can cardamom or caraway seeds. Use the egg yolk to brush the tops of the cookies before baking.

Decorating Ideas and Tips

Cookies are fine if served plain, but they can be spectacular if decorated or iced, and there are many ways of doing this.

Before or After?

Perhaps the easiest way to decorate is before baking. Place the rolled out cookies onto the baking sheet, then simply sprinkle a few slivered almonds or chopped nuts over each and lightly sprinkle with either superfine sugar or turbinado (raw) sugar. Bake in the oven until golden.

After baking, make this simple icing, which can be left white or colored with edible food coloring. Spread it over the top of the cookies, or place a cutter, such as a holly leaf, in the center of the cookie and fill the cutter with a little of the icing. Let stand until almost set before removing the cutter.

Glacé Icing

⅓ cup confectioners' sugar
1–2 tbsp. hot water

Sift the confectioners' sugar into a small mixing bowl and slowly beat in some of the hot water. Beat well. If necessary, use more water to mix the icing to a spreadable consistency and use immediately. Use a blunt knife or spatula to spread the icing over the cookies.

Icing Tips

- Before the icing sets, sprinkle with a few sugar strands or chocolate sprinkles. Children love jelly babies and gum drops, so place a few on top, if desired.

- If liked, the icing can be flavored by the addition of an extract, or replace 1 tablespoon of the sugar with sifted unsweetened cocoa. Alternatively, use lemon or orange juice in place of the water.

- A great decoration that is also easy to do is to ice the cookies, then use some letter cutters on top (one per cookie) to mark out people's names. This is ideal for kids' birthday parties.

- If liked, make the icing slightly thicker, place in a pastry bag fitted with a writing tip, and pipe names on each cookie. Let stand to set before storing.

Sprinkling Confectioners' Sugar

You could also place a cutter in the center of a cookie and, using a tiny strainer, such as a tea strainer, sift the inside of the cutter with a thick layer of confectioners' sugar. I would suggest that this decoration is done just before serving, otherwise the pattern could be disturbed if stored first.

Rolled Fondant Icing

You can also use a cutter to decorate your cookies with ready-to-use rolled fondant shapes. This icing is available from specialty cake shops and on the Internet in white, ivory, red, green, black, and blue. You will need a small amount of apricot glaze to stick the shapes on the cookies.

Apricot Glaze

¼ cup apricot preserve
1 tbsp. lemon juice or water

Heat the preserve and juice or water together and, when hot, remove from the heat and push through a fine strainer. Use a pastry brush to apply to either the top of the cookie or to the underside of the shape to be attached.

Using Fondant

Fondant can be used very easily. Decide on the color of fondant you want to use and the shape. When choosing the shape, use small cutters instead of large. Roll out the fondant on a surface sprinkled with a little confectioners' sugar or cornstarch and cut out the shapes. Brush the tops of the cookies with a little apricot glaze, then place the shapes in position. Let stand for a few minutes for the glaze to set before serving.

Buttercream and Chocolate

Cookies can also be decorated with buttercream or melted chocolate. Both buttercream and melted chocolate can be used to sandwich cookies together, if liked. These will need to be eaten quickly and will not store well, because the filling will make the cookies turn soggy quickly. However, it is well worth doing, because they taste absolutely delicious.

Buttercream

6 tbsp. unsalted butter, softened
1⅓ cups confectioners' sugar, sifted
1–2 tsp., or to taste, flavoring of choice, such as
    vanilla extract, lemon zest, or orange zest

Beat the butter until very creamy, then gradually beat in the confectioners' sugar and flavoring until a thick, spreadable frosting is formed. Use as required.

Cookies from Around the World

Apart from the everyday cookies, there are many speciality types that can easily be made at home. These include Australian Anzac Cookies, Czechoslovakian Cookies, Sablés, Almond Petit Fours, Palmiers, and Swedish Gingerbread.

Anzac Cookies

These cookies date back to World War I—the word "Anzac" stands for the "Australian and New Zealand Army Corps." They are said to have been sent to soldiers by concerned wives to provide some nutritional food that did not spoil easily. The cookies are still a favorite with many.

Makes 25–30

1 cup rolled oats
⅔ cup all-purpose flour
1 cup unsweetened dry flaked coconut
⅔ cup unbleached superfine sugar
1 tsp. baking soda
7 tbsp. unsalted butter, melted
2 tbsp. light corn syrup, warmed

Preheat the oven to 350°F about 10 minutes before baking. Place the oats, flour, and coconut into a mixing bowl and stir in the sugar.

Dissolve the baking soda in 2 tablespoons boiling water, stirring until completely dissolved.

Make a well in the center of the dry ingredients, then stir in the melted butter with the dissolved baking soda and the corn syrup. Mix well, then place mounds of about 2 teaspoons each onto lightly oiled or lined baking sheets, leaving room for expansion. Bake in the preheated oven for 8–10 minutes until golden. Remove from the oven and let cool before transferring to wire racks.

Helpful Hint Making a well in the center of dry ingredients when adding the wet ingredients makes it far easier to combine the two, and ensures that they are well blended.

Czechoslovakian Cookies

These cookies are still popular, especially around Christmas time. Czechoslovakian (now Czech or Slovakian, of course) families begin their Christmas earlier than in North America, and this recipe is one they would make around St. Nicholas' Feast day on December 6.

Makes 12–14

1 cup unsalted butter, softened
1 cup plus 2 tbsp. superfine sugar
2 extra-large egg yolks
1¾ cups all-purpose flour
1 cup walnuts, chopped
3 tbsp. strawberry preserves

Preheat the oven to 350°F about 10 minutes before baking. Lightly oil a 10 x 8-inch baking pan (it needs to be about 2 inches deep). Beat the butter and sugar together until creamy and very light and fluffy, then gradually beat in the egg yolks, then the flour, and then the walnuts.

Using a little extra flour, press half the mixture into the oiled baking pan and then spread the top with the preserves. Cover with the remaining dough. Bake in the preheated oven for 40–50 minutes until golden, remove from the oven, and let cool on wire racks. When cold, cut into squares.

Helpful Hint Other flavors of preserves can be used, if preferred, such as raspberry or apricot. If using apricot, you could add some finely chopped plumped dried apricots.

Lemon & Cardamom Sablés

These cookies are crisp to eat and crammed full of flavor, with a wonderful melt-in-the mouth texture. Perfect to serve with summer desserts, such as mixed berry compote or simply fresh berries.

Makes 18–20

4–6 green cardamom pods
1 cup all-purpose flour, plus extra (2 tbsp.) for rolling
⅓ cup plus 1 tbsp. confectioners' sugar, sifted
finely grated zest of 1 large lemon, preferably organic
7 tbsp. unsalted butter, softened
1 large egg yolk
1 tbsp. strained lemon juice

Preheat the oven to 350°F about 10 minutes before baking. Lightly oil two or three baking sheets. Crack the cardamom pods and scoop out the seeds. Set aside the seeds.

Sift the flour and confectioners' sugar into a mixing bowl and stir in the cardamom, zest, butter, egg yolk, and lemon juice. Stir, then beat to form a soft dough. Wrap and chill for 30 minutes.

Roll the dough out on a lightly floured surface to about ¼ inch thick. Cut out rounds about 3 inches in diameter and place on the oiled baking sheets. Bake in the preheated oven for 8–10 minutes until golden. Cool for 1–2 minutes before transferring to wire racks. Serve when cold.

Helpful Hint For a wicked treat, melt equal quantities of dark chocolate and heavy cream together. Stir until smooth. Let stand until cold, beating occasionally. When cold, it will be very thick. Beat well to make a soft chocolate cream known as chocolate ganache. Sandwich two cookies together using the ganache.

Almond Petit Fours

These little delights, originally from France, are perfect for almost every occasion, whether served with coffee in the morning or after dinner, with tea in the afternoon, or as a quick boost of energy in the evening. Being really easy to make and bake, they have to be added to a list of favorite recipes.

Makes 20–24

2 extra-large egg whites
⅔ cup superfine sugar
1 tsp. almond extract
1¾ cups plus 1 tbsp. ground almonds

Preheat the oven to 300°F about 10 minutes before baking. Line two or three baking sheets with nonstick parchment paper or rice paper. Whisk the egg whites in a clean, grease-free bowl until stiff, then gradually stir in the superfine sugar, a spoonful at a time. Whisk well before adding the next spoonful.

When all the sugar has been added, whisk in the almond extract. Add the ground almonds and stir lightly until blended.

Either place small spoonfuls onto the prepared baking sheets, or spoon into a large pastry bag fitted with a large star tip and pipe small rosettes onto the sheets. Bake in the preheated oven for 15–20 minutes until pale golden. Cool before removing from the baking sheets. Serve cold. Store in an airtight container.

Helpful Hint If liked, place a small piece of angelica, candied cherry, or nut on top of each petit four before baking. Try replacing the almond extract with rose water.

Cheese Palmiers

These also come from France, and can be served on a variety of occasions. However, there is one big difference—these are savory.

Makes about 12

8 oz. store-bought puff pastry
all-purpose flour, for rolling
1¼ cups finely grated strong cheese, such as Gruyère, sharp cheddar, or Parmesan
1 large egg, beaten

Preheat the oven to 425°F about 15 minutes before baking. Lightly oil two or three baking sheets. Roll the pastry out on a lightly floured surface to an oblong about 20 inches long. Sprinkle with 2–3 tablespoons of the cheese. Fold the long sides over to the center until they meet. Press together. Sprinkle with more cheese. Fold the sides to the center again, press down, and sprinkle with more cheese. Place the two folded sections together and press firmly.

Using a sharp knife, cut into thin slices and place cut-side down on the baking sheets. Brush with beaten egg and sprinkle with any remaining cheese. Bake in the preheated oven for 6–7 minutes until golden. Turn the cookies over and lightly brush with the egg. Continue to bake for an additional 6–7 minutes until golden. Remove from the oven and transfer to a wire rack. Let stand until cold before serving.

Helpful Hint A sweet version can be made, if liked. Simply replace the grated cheese with superfine sugar. Two sweet palmiers can be sandwiched together with whipped cream.

Langues de Chat

Translated from the French, this means "cat tongues," so called most probably because of their shape. They are very easy to make and can be served plain or dipped in icing or chocolate, whichever you prefer.

Makes 12–14

4 tbsp. unsalted butter, softened

¼ cup superfine sugar

1 large egg, beaten

⅓ cup plus 1 tbsp. self-rising flour

1 tsp. vanilla extract

2 tbsp. cornstarch

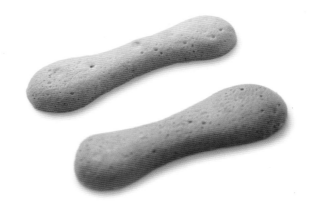

Preheat the oven to 425°F about 15 minutes before baking. Lightly oil two baking sheets. Cream the butter and sugar together until blended, then beat in the egg together with a little flour. Add the vanilla extract, stir in the remaining flour and the cornstarch; beat until smooth.

Place in a pastry bag fitted with a large plain tip. Pipe short lengths on the baking sheets. Bake in the preheated oven for 5–6 minutes until the edges are turning golden. Remove from the oven and let cool for 2–3 minutes before transferring to a wire rack. Serve when cold.

Helpful Hint If liked, the cookies can have both ends dipped in melted chocolate and sandwiched together with either whipped cream or buttercream.

Swedish Gingerbread Cookies

These Swedish gingerbread cookies, or "pepparkakor," play an important part at Christmas. They are made for the first Sunday of Advent and herald the start of the Christmas season.

Makes 20–24

8 tbsp. unsalted butter

½ cup turbinado (raw) sugar or light brown sugar

¾ cup plus 2 tbsp. light corn syrup or molasses

1 tsp. ground ginger

1½ tsp. ground cloves or allspice

2 tsp. baking soda

1 large egg, beaten

3⅔ cups all-purpose flour

Preheat the oven to 325°F about 10 minutes before baking. Lightly oil two or three baking sheets and set aside. Place the butter in a large, heavy saucepan together with the sugar, corn syrup or molasses, spices, and baking soda. Slowly bring to a boil, stirring frequently.

Stir until blended, then remove from the heat. Let cool a little, then beat in the egg with 2 tablespoons of the flour. Beat well. Continue to beat in the flour, beating well after each addition.

When all the flour has been added, place on a surface dusted with a little extra flour. Knead until a smooth and pliable dough is formed—one that will roll out easily. Cut the dough in half or quarters and roll out the first batch thinly. Using cutters, cut into shapes and place on the baking sheets. Repeat with the remaining dough.

Bake in the preheated oven for 10–15 minutes until firm on top. Remove and let cool for 1 minute before transferring to a wire rack. If liked, decorate with icing and serve.

Classic Cookies

Chocolate Chip Cookies

Makes 30

½ cup plus 1 tbsp. (1⅛ sticks) butter
¼ cup superfine sugar
⅓ cup packed dark brown sugar
1 large egg, beaten
½ tsp. vanilla extract
1 cup all-purpose flour
½ tsp. baking soda
¾ cup semisweet dark or milk chocolate chips

1. Preheat the oven to 350°F. Lightly butter three to four large baking sheets with 1 tablespoon of the butter. Place the remaining butter and both sugars in a food processor, and blend until smooth. Add the egg and vanilla extract, and blend briefly. Alternatively, cream the butter and sugars together in a large bowl, then beat in the egg with the vanilla extract.

2. If using a food processor, scrape out the batter with a spatula, and place the batter into a large bowl. Sift the flour and baking soda together, then fold into the creamed batter. When the batter is blended thoroughly, stir in the chocolate chips.

3. Drop heaping teaspoons of the batter onto the prepared baking sheets. Make sure they are spaced well apart, because they will spread during cooking. Bake in the preheated oven for 10–12 minutes until lightly golden.

4. Let cool for a few seconds, then, using a spatula, transfer to a wire rack and cool completely. The cookies are best eaten when just cooked but can be stored in an airtight container for a few days.

Chewy Choc & Nut Cookies

Makes 18

1 tbsp. butter
4 large egg whites
3 cups confectioners' sugar
¼ cup unsweetened cocoa
2 tbsp. all-purpose flour
1 tsp. instant coffee powder
1 cup finely chopped walnuts

1. Preheat the oven to 350°F. Lightly butter several cookie sheets with the butter, and line with a sheet of nonstick parchment paper. Place the egg whites in a large, grease-free bowl, and beat with an electric mixer until the egg whites are very frothy.

2. Add the sugar, unsweetened cocoa, flour, and coffee powder, and beat again until they are blended thoroughly. Add 1 tablespoon water, and beat on the highest speed until the mixture is very thick. Fold in the walnuts.

3. Place tablespoons of the batter onto the prepared cookie sheets, leaving plenty of space between them, as they expand greatly during cooking.

4. Bake in the preheated oven for 12–15 minutes until the tops are firm, golden, and quite cracked. Let cool for 30 seconds, then transfer to a wire rack and let cool. Store in an airtight container.

White Chocolate Cookies

Makes about 24

½ cup plus 1 tbsp. (1⅛ sticks) butter
3 tbsp. sugar
⅓ cup firmly packed dark brown sugar
1 large egg
1 cup all-purpose flour
½ tsp. baking soda
few drops vanilla extract
5 oz. white chocolate
½ cup shelled whole hazelnuts

1. Preheat the oven to 350°F. Lightly butter several cookie sheets with 1 tablespoon of the butter. Place the remaining butter with both sugars into a large bowl and beat with a wooden spoon or an electric mixer until soft and fluffy.

2. Beat the egg, then gradually beat it into the creamed mixture. Sift the flour and the baking soda together, then carefully fold into the creamed mixture with a few drops of vanilla extract.

3. Coarsely chop the chocolate and hazelnuts into small pieces, add to the bowl, and gently stir into the batter. Mix together lightly to blend.

4. Spoon heaping teaspoons of the batter onto the prepared cookie sheets, making sure that there is plenty of space in between them, as they will spread a lot during cooking.

5. Bake the cookies in the preheated oven for 10 minutes, or until golden, then remove from the oven and let cool for 1 minute. Using a spatula, carefully transfer to a wire rack and let cool completely. The cookies are best eaten on the day they are made. Store in an airtight container.

Chocolate & Hazelnut Cookies

Makes 12

¾ **cup blanched hazelnuts**
⅔ **cup superfine sugar**
4 **tbsp. unsalted butter**
pinch salt
5 **tsp. unsweetened cocoa**
3 **tbsp. heavy cream**
2 **extra-large egg whites**
2 **tbsp. all-purpose flour**
2 **tbsp. rum**
3 **oz. white chocolate**

1. Preheat the oven to 350°F. Lightly grease and flour two or three baking sheets. Chop ¼ cup of the hazelnuts and set aside. Blend the remaining hazelnuts with the sugar in a food processor until finely ground. Add the butter to the processor bowl and then blend until pale and creamy.

2. Add the salt, unsweetened cocoa, and the heavy cream, and mix well. Scrape the batter into a bowl with a spatula, and stir in the egg whites. Sift the flour, then stir into the batter together with the rum.

3. Spoon heaping tablespoons of the batter onto the baking sheet and sprinkle over the chopped hazelnuts. Bake in the preheated oven for 5–7 minutes until firm. Remove the cookies from the oven and let cool for 1–2 minutes. Using a spatula, transfer to wire racks and let cool.

4. When the cookies are cool, melt the chocolate in a heatproof bowl set over a saucepan of simmering water. Stir until smooth, then drizzle a little of the chocolate over the top of each cookie. Let dry on a wire rack before serving.

Chocolate & Almond Cookies

Makes 18–20

½ cup plus 1 tbsp. (1⅛ sticks) butter
⅔ cup confectioners' sugar
1 large egg, beaten
1 tbsp. milk
1 tbsp. grated lemon zest
2¼ cups all-purpose flour
1 cup chopped blanched almonds
4 oz. semisweet dark chocolate
¾ cup toasted flaked or slivered almonds

1. Preheat the oven to 400°F. Lightly grease several cookie sheets. Cream the butter and confectioners' sugar together until light and fluffy, then gradually beat in the egg, beating well after each addition. When all the egg has been added, stir in the milk and lemon zest.

2. Sift the flour, then stir into the batter together with the chopped almonds to form a smooth and pliable dough. Wrap in plastic wrap and chill in the refrigerator for 2 hours.

3. Roll the dough out on a lightly floured surface into a large oblong shape about ¼ inch thick. Cut into strips, about 2½ inches long and 1½ inches wide, and place on the prepared cookie sheets.

4. Bake in the preheated oven for 15 minutes, or until golden, then remove from the oven and let cool for a few minutes. Transfer to a wire rack and let cool completely.

5. Melt the chocolate in a small, heatproof bowl set over a saucepan of simmering water. Alternatively, melt the chocolate in the microwave, according to the manufacturer's directions, until smooth. Spread the chocolate thickly over the cookies, sprinkle over the toasted flaked or slivered almonds, and let set before serving.

Chocolate & Nut Refrigerator Cookies

Makes 18

½ cup plus 3 tbsp. (1⅜ sticks) salted butter
⅔ cup firmly packed dark brown sugar
2 tbsp. granulated sugar
1 large egg, beaten
1¼ cups all-purpose flour
½ tsp. baking soda
¼ cup unsweetened cocoa
1 cup finely chopped pecans

1. Preheat the oven to 375°F. Lightly grease several large cookie sheets with 1 tablespoon of the butter. Cream the remaining butter and both sugars in a large bowl until light and fluffy, then gradually beat in the egg.

2. Sift the flour, baking soda, and unsweetened cocoa together, then gradually fold into the creamed batter together with the chopped pecans. Mix thoroughly until a smooth but stiff dough is formed.

3. Place the dough on a lightly floured surface and roll into sausage shapes about 2 inches in diameter. Wrap in plastic wrap and chill in the refrigerator for at least 12 hours, or preferably overnight.

4. Cut the dough into thin slices and place on the prepared cookie sheets. Bake in the preheated oven for 8–10 minutes until firm. Remove from the oven and let cool slightly. Using a spatula, transfer to a wire rack to cool. Store in an airtight container.

Golden Honey Fork Cookies

Makes 20–24

½ cup (1 stick) diced butter or margarine
heaping ½ cup packed light brown sugar
1 large egg, beaten
½ tsp. vanilla extract
2 tbsp. honey
1⅔ cups all-purpose flour
½ tsp. baking powder
½ tsp. ground cinnamon

1. Preheat the oven to 350°F. Grease two cookie sheets.

2. Place the butter and sugar in a bowl and beat together until light and fluffy. Beat in the egg a little at a time, and then beat in the vanilla extract and honey.

3. Sift the flour, baking powder, and cinnamon into the bowl and fold into the mixture with a large metal spoon.

4. Put heaping teaspoons of the mixture onto the prepared cookie sheets, leaving room for them to spread out during baking. Press the top of each round with the tines of a fork to make a light indentation.

5. Bake for 10–12 minutes until golden. Cool for 2 minutes on the cookie sheets, then transfer to a wire rack to cool completely.

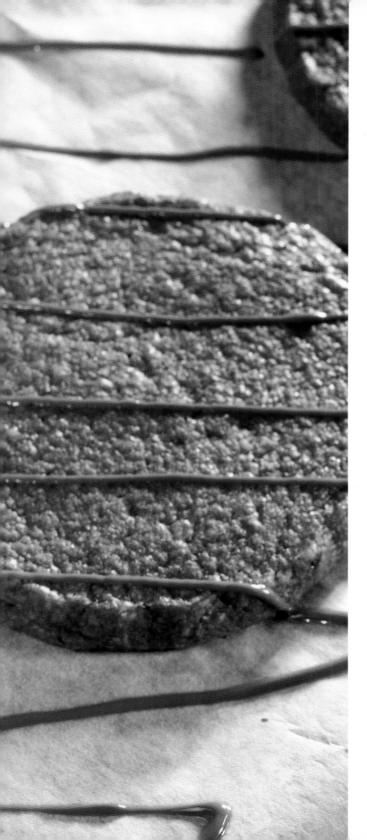

Chocolate Shortcake

Makes 30–32

1 cup (2 sticks) unsalted butter, softened
1¼ cups confectioners' sugar, sifted, plus
 extra to decorate
1 tsp. vanilla extract
2¼ cups all-purpose flour
¼ cup unsweetened cocoa
¼ tsp. salt

1. Preheat the oven to 325°F. Lightly grease several cookie
   sheets and line with nonstick parchment paper. Place the
   butter, confectioners' sugar, and vanilla extract together in
   a food processor and blend briefly until smooth.
   Alternatively, using a wooden spoon, cream the butter,
   confectioners' sugar, and vanilla extract in a bowl.

2. Sift the flour, cocoa, and salt together, then either add to
   the food processor bowl and blend quickly to form a
   dough, or add to the bowl and, using your hands, mix
   together until a smooth dough is formed.

3. Turn the dough out onto a clean board lined with plastic
   wrap. Place another sheet of plastic wrap over the top and
   roll the dough out until it is ½ inch thick. Transfer the
   whole board to the refrigerator and chill for 1½–2 hours.

4. Remove the top piece of plastic wrap and use a 2-inch
   cutter to cut the dough into 30–32 rounds. Place the
   rounds on the prepared cookie sheets and bake in the
   preheated oven for about 15 minutes until firm.

5. Cool for 1 minute, then, using a spatula, carefully remove
   the shortcakes from the parchment paper and transfer to a
   wire rack. Let cool completely. Sprinkle the shortcakes
   with confectioners' sugar before serving. Store in an
   airtight container for a few days.

Melting Moments

Makes 16

½ cup (1 stick) softened butter
⅓ cup superfine sugar
½ tsp. vanilla extract
1¼ cups self-rising flour
pinch salt
1 medium egg or ½ large egg, beaten
heaping ¼ cup rolled oats
4 candied cherries, quartered

1. Preheat the oven to 350°F. Grease two cookie sheets.

2. Beat the butter until light and fluffy, then beat in the
   superfine sugar and vanilla extract. Sift the flour and salt
   into a bowl. Add the egg and mix to a soft dough.

3. Break the dough into 16 pieces and roll each piece into a
   ball. Spread the oats out on a small, flat bowl or plate.
   Roll each ball in the oats to coat them all over, without
   flattening them.

4. Place a cherry quarter in the center of each ball, then
   place on the cookie sheets, spaced well apart. Bake for
   about 15 minutes until risen and golden. Remove from
   the cookie sheets with a palette knife and cool on a
   wire rack.

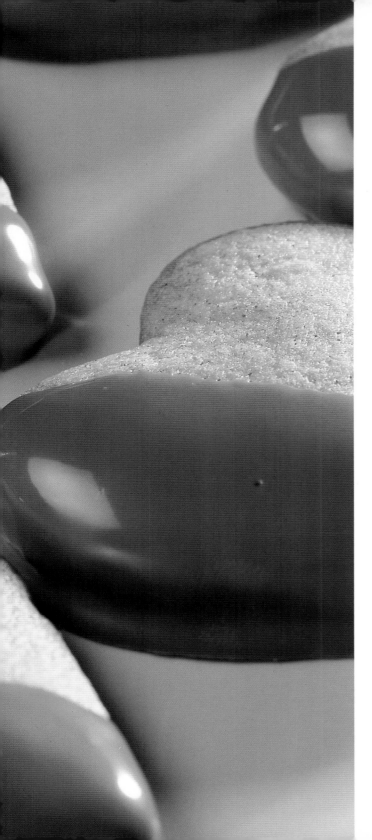

Honey & Chocolate Hearts

Makes about 20

4½ tbsp. superfine sugar
1 tbsp. butter
⅓ cup thick honey
1 medium egg, beaten
pinch salt
1 tbsp. mixed peel or chopped candied ginger
¼ tsp. ground cinnamon
pinch ground cloves
2 cups all-purpose flour, sifted
½ tsp. baking powder, sifted
3 oz. milk chocolate

1. Preheat the oven to 425°F. Lightly grease two baking sheets. Heat the sugar, butter, and honey together in a small saucepan until everything has melted and the mixture is completely smooth.

2. Remove from the heat and stir until slightly cooled, then add the beaten egg with the salt, and beat well. Stir in the mixed peel or candied ginger, the ground cinnamon, ground cloves, flour, and baking powder, and mix until a dough is formed. Wrap in plastic wrap and chill in the refrigerator for 45 minutes.

3. Place the chilled dough on a lightly floured surface, roll out to about ¼-inch thickness and cut out small heart shapes. Place onto the prepared baking sheets and bake in the preheated oven for 8–10 minutes. Remove from the oven and let cool slightly. Using a spatula, transfer to a wire rack and let cool.

4. Melt the chocolate in a heatproof bowl set over a saucepan of simmering water. Alternatively, melt the chocolate in the microwave, according to the manufacturer's directions, until smooth. Dip one half of each cookie in the melted chocolate. Let set before serving.

Chocolate Orange Cookies

Makes 30

3½ oz. semisweet dark chocolate
½ cup (1 stick) butter
½ cup superfine sugar
pinch salt
1 large egg, beaten
3 tbsp. grated orange zest
1¼ cups all-purpose flour
1 tsp. baking powder
1 cup confectioners' sugar
1–2 tbsp. orange juice

1. Preheat the oven to 400°F. Lightly grease several baking sheets. Coarsely grate the chocolate and set aside. Beat the butter and sugar together until creamy. Add the salt, beaten egg, and half the orange zest, and beat again.

2. Sift the flour and baking powder, add to the bowl with the chocolate, and beat to form a dough. Shape into a ball, wrap in plastic wrap, and chill in the refrigerator for 2 hours.

3. Roll the dough out on a lightly floured surface to ¼-inch thickness and cut into 2-inch rounds. Place the rounds on the prepared baking sheets, leaving room for expansion. Bake in the preheated oven for 10–12 minutes until firm. Remove the cookies from the oven and let cool slightly. Using a spatula, transfer to a wire rack and let cool.

4. Sift the confectioners' sugar into a small bowl and stir in sufficient orange juice to make a smooth, spreadable icing. Spread the icing over the cookies, leave until almost set, then sprinkle on the remaining grated orange zest before serving.

Ginger Snaps

Makes 40

1⅓ cups (2¾ sticks) butter or margarine, softened
1 cup light brown sugar
3 tbsp. molasses
1 large egg
3½ cups all-purpose flour
2 tsp. baking soda
½ tsp. salt
1 tsp. ground ginger
1 tsp. ground cloves
1 tsp. ground cinnamon
4 tbsp. granulated sugar

1. Preheat the oven to 375°F. Lightly grease a baking sheet.

2. Cream together the butter or margarine and the sugar until light and fluffy.

3. Warm the molasses in the microwave for 30–40 seconds, then add gradually to the butter mixture with the egg. Beat until well mixed.

4. In a separate bowl, sift the flour, baking soda, salt, ground ginger, ground cloves, and cinnamon. Add to the butter mixture and mix together to form a firm dough.

5. Chill in the refrigerator for 1 hour. Shape the dough into small balls, and roll in the granulated sugar. Place well apart on the greased baking sheet.

6. Sprinkle the baking sheet with a little water and transfer to the preheated oven. Bake for 12 minutes until golden and crisp. Transfer to a wire rack to cool, and serve.

Chocolate & Vanilla Rings

Makes 26

¾ cup (1½ sticks) softened butter
⅔ cup superfine sugar
few drops vanilla extract
2 cups all-purpose flour
2 tbsp. plus 2 tsp. unsweetened cocoa
¼ cup ground almonds

1. Preheat the oven to 350°F and grease two
   cookie sheets.

2. Put the butter and sugar in a bowl and beat until light
   and fluffy. Add the vanilla extract, sift in the flour, and
   mix to a soft dough. Divide the dough in two and add
   the unsweetened cocoa to one half and the almonds to
   the other.

3. Knead each piece of dough separately into a smooth
   ball, wrap, and chill for 30 minutes. Divide each piece
   into 26 pieces. Take one dark and one light ball and roll
   each separately into ropes about 5 inches long, using
   your fingers.

4. Twist the ropes together to form a circlet and pinch the
   ends together. Repeat with the remaining dough and
   place on a greased cookie sheet. Bake for 12–14 minutes
   until risen and firm. Remove to cool on a wire rack.

Lemon Butter Cookies

Makes 14–18

¾ cup (1½ sticks) softened butter
⅓ cup superfine sugar
1⅓ cups all-purpose flour
⅔ cup cornstarch
zest of 1 lemon, finely grated
2 tbsp. superfine sugar, to decorate

1. Preheat the oven to 325°F. Grease two cookie sheets.
   Place the butter into a bowl and beat together with the
   sugar until light and fluffy.

2. Sift in the flour and cornstarch, add the lemon zest, and
   mix together with a flat-bladed knife to form a soft dough.

3. Place the dough on a lightly floured surface, knead lightly,
   and roll out thinly. Use cookie cutters to cut out fancy
   shapes, then roll out the trimmings to make more
   cookies. Carefully lift each cookie onto a cookie sheet
   with a palette knife, then prick lightly with a fork.

4. Bake for 12–15 minutes. Cool on the cookie sheets for 5
   minutes, then place on a wire rack. Once completely
   cool, dust with superfine sugar.

Oatmeal Raisin Cookies

Makes 24

1½ cups all-purpose flour
2 cups rolled oats
1 tsp. ground ginger
½ tsp. baking powder
½ tsp. baking soda
½ cup light brown sugar
⅓ cup raisins
1 large egg, lightly beaten
⅔ cup vegetable or sunflower oil
4 tbsp. milk

1. Preheat the oven to 400°F. Lightly grease a baking sheet.

2. Mix together the flour, oats, ground ginger, baking
   powder, baking soda, sugar, and raisins in a large bowl.

3. In another bowl, mix the egg, oil, and milk together.
   Make a well in the center of the dry ingredients, and pour
   in the egg mixture. Mix until you have a soft, but not
   sticky, dough.

4. Place spoonfuls of the dough well apart on the greased
   baking sheet, and flatten the tops down slightly with the
   tines of a fork.

5. Transfer the cookies to the preheated oven, and bake for
   10–12 minutes until golden.

6. Remove from the oven, let cool on the tray for 2–3
   minutes, then transfer the cookies to a wire rack to cool.
   Serve when cold, or store in an airtight container.

Oatmeal Coconut Cookies

Makes 40

1 cup (2 sticks) butter or margarine
½ cup light brown sugar
½ cup superfine sugar
1 extra-large egg, lightly beaten
1 tsp. vanilla extract
2 cups all-purpose flour
1 tsp. baking powder
½ tsp. baking soda
1¼ cups rolled oats
1 cup unsweetened shredded dry coconut

1. Preheat the oven to 350°F. Lightly grease a baking sheet.

2. Cream together the butter or margarine and the sugars until light and fluffy. Gradually stir in the egg and vanilla extract, and beat until well blended.

3. Sift together the flour, baking powder, and baking soda in another bowl. Add to the butter-and-sugar mixture, and beat together until smooth. Fold in the rolled oats and coconut with a metal spoon or rubber spatula.

4. Roll heaping teaspoonfuls of the mixture into balls and place on the baking sheet about 2 inches apart, and flatten each ball slightly with the heel of the hand.

5. Transfer to the preheated oven and bake for 12–15 minutes until just golden.

6. Remove from the oven and transfer the cookies to a wire rack to cool completely, and serve.

Whipped Shortbread

Makes 36

1 cup (2 sticks) softened
 butter
⅔ cup confectioners' sugar
1½ cups all-purpose flour

To decorate:
sprinkles
sugar strands
chocolate chips
silver balls
5 tbsp. confectioners'
 sugar
2–3 tsp. lemon juice

1. Preheat the oven to 350°F. Lightly grease a baking sheet.

2. Cream the butter and confectioners' sugar together until fluffy. Gradually add the flour and continue beating for an additional 2–3 minutes until it is smooth and light.

3. Roll into balls and place on a baking sheet. Or, for a smarter-looking cookie, spoon the mixture into a decorating bag fitted with a large star tip and pipe the cookies onto the baking sheet. Cover half the dough mixture with half the sprinkles, sugar strands, chocolate chips, or silver balls. Keep the other half plain.

4. Bake in the preheated oven for 6–8 minutes until the bottoms are lightly browned. Remove from the oven, and transfer to a wire rack to cool.

5. To decorate further, sift the confectioners' sugar into a small bowl. Add the lemon juice, and blend until a smooth icing forms. Using a small spoon, swirl the icing over the cooled plain cookies. Decorate with extra sprinkles, chocolate chips, or silver balls, and serve.

Shortbread Thumbs

Makes 12

1 cup self-rising flour
½ cup (1 stick) butter, softened
2 tbsp. shortening
¼ cup granulated sugar
¼ cup sifted cornstarch
5 tbsp. sifted unsweetened cocoa
1 cup confectioners' sugar
6 assorted colored candied cherries, rinsed, dried, and halved

1. Preheat the oven to 300°F. Lightly grease two baking sheets. Sift the flour into a large bowl, cut ¾ stick of the butter and the shortening into small cubes, add to the flour, then, using your fingertips, rub in until the batter resembles fine bread crumbs.

2. Stir in the granulated sugar, sifted cornstarch, and 4 tablespoons of the unsweetened cocoa, and bring the batter together with your hand to form a soft and pliable dough.

3. Place on a lightly floured surface and shape into 12 small balls. Place onto the baking sheets at least 2 inches apart, then press each one with a clean thumb to make a dent.

4. Bake in the preheated oven for 20–25 minutes until light golden brown. Remove from the oven and let cool for 1–2 minutes. Transfer to a wire rack and leave until cold.

5. Sift the confectioners' sugar and the remaining cocoa into a bowl, and add the remaining softened butter. Blend to form a smooth and spreadable frosting with 1–2 tablespoons hot water. Spread a little frosting over the top of each cookie and place half a cherry on each. Let set before serving.

Gingerbread Cookies

Makes 20 large or 28 small

1¾ cups all-purpose flour, plus extra for dusting
½ tsp. ground ginger
½ tsp. allspice
½ tsp. baking soda
6 tbsp. butter
2 tbsp. corn syrup
1 tbsp. molasses
⅓ cup packed dark brown sugar
heaping ⅓ cup confectioners' sugar, to decorate

1. Preheat the oven to 350°F and grease two cookie sheets.
   Sift the flour, spices, and baking soda into a bowl.

2. Place the butter, syrup, molasses, and sugar in a heavy pan
   with 1 tablespoon water and heat gently until every grain
   of sugar has dissolved and the butter has melted. Cool for
   5 minutes, then pour the melted mixture into the dry
   ingredients and mix to a soft dough.

3. Let the dough stand, covered, for 30 minutes. Roll out
   the dough on a lightly floured surface to an ⅛-inch
   thickness and cut out fancy shapes. Gather up the
   trimmings and re-roll the dough, cutting out more
   shapes. Place on the cookie sheets using a spatula, and
   bake for about 10 minutes until golden and firm. Be
   careful not to overcook, because the cookies will
   brown quickly.

4. Decorate the cookies by mixing the confectioners' sugar
   with enough water to make a piping consistency. Place
   the icing in a small paper pastry bag with the end snipped
   away, and pipe faces and decorations onto the cookies.

Viennese Fingers

Makes 28

1 cup (2 sticks)
 softened butter
⅔ cup confectioners' sugar
1 large egg, beaten
1 tsp. vanilla extract
2¼ cups all-purpose flour
½ tsp. baking powder

To decorate:

4 tbsp. strained apricot jelly
8 oz. semisweet dark
 chocolate

1. Preheat the oven to 350°F. Grease two cookie sheets. Put the butter and confectioners' sugar in a bowl and beat together until soft and fluffy.

2. Beat in the egg and vanilla extract with 1 tablespoon of the flour. Sift in the remaining flour and the baking powder, and beat with a wooden spoon to make a soft dough.

3. Place the mixture in a pastry bag fitted with a large star tip and pipe into 2½-inch lengths on the cookie sheets. Bake for 15–20 minutes until pale golden and firm, then transfer to a wire rack to cool.

4. When cold, thinly spread one flat side of a cookie with apricot jelly and sandwich together with another cookie.

5. To decorate the cookies, break the chocolate into squares and place in a heatproof bowl and stand this over a pan of simmering water. Stir until the chocolate has melted, then dip the ends of the cookies into the chocolate to coat. Let stand on a wire rack for 1 hour until set.

Special
Cookies

Cantuccini

Makes 24

2¼ cups all-purpose flour
1 cup superfine sugar
½ tsp. baking powder
½ tsp. vanilla extract
2 large eggs
1 large egg yolk
5 tbsp. mixed almonds and hazelnuts, toasted and
  coarsely chopped
1 tsp. whole aniseed
1 large egg yolk mixed with 1 tbsp. water, to glaze
Vin Santo or coffee, to serve

1. Preheat the oven to 350°F. Line a large baking sheet with
   nonstick parchment paper. Place the flour, sugar, baking
   powder, vanilla extract, whole eggs, and the egg yolk into
   a food processor, and blend until the mixture forms a ball,
   scraping down the sides once or twice. Turn the mixture
   out onto a lightly floured surface, and knead in the
   chopped nuts and aniseed.

2. Divide the paste into three pieces and roll into logs about
   1½ inches wide. Place the logs onto the baking sheet at
   least 2 inches apart. Brush lightly with the egg yolk
   beaten with water, and bake in the preheated oven for
   30–35 minutes.

3. Remove from the oven and reduce the oven temperature
   to 300°F. Cut the logs diagonally into 1-inch slices and lay
   cut-side down on the baking sheet. Return to the oven
   for an additional 30–40 minutes until dry and firm. Cool
   the cookies on a wire rack, and store in a large airtight
   container. Serve with Vin Santo or coffee.

Almond & Pistachio Biscotti

Makes 12

1 cup ground almonds
½ cup shelled pistachios
½ cup blanched almonds
2 large eggs
1 large egg yolk
⅔ cup confectioners' sugar
2 cups all-purpose flour
1 tsp. baking powder
pinch salt
3 tsp. lemon zest

1. Preheat the oven to 350°F. Line a large baking sheet with nonstick parchment paper. Toast the ground almonds and whole nuts lightly, and set aside until cool.

2. Beat together the eggs, egg yolk, and confectioners' sugar until thick, then beat in the flour, baking powder, and salt. Add the lemon zest, ground almonds, and nuts, and mix to form a slightly sticky dough.

3. Turn the dough onto a lightly floured surface, and, using lightly floured hands, form into a log measuring approximately 12 inches long. Place down the center of the prepared baking sheet and transfer to the preheated oven. Cook for 20 minutes.

4. Remove from the oven and increase the oven temperature to 400°F. Cut the log diagonally into 1-inch slices. Return to the baking sheet cut-side down, and cook for an additional 10–15 minutes until golden, turning once after 10 minutes. Let cool on a wire rack, and store in a large airtight container.

Chocolate Macaroon Cookies

Makes 20

2½ oz. semisweet dark chocolate
1 cup ground almonds
½ cup superfine sugar
¼ tsp. almond extract
1 tbsp. unsweetened cocoa
2 large egg whites
1 tbsp. confectioners' sugar

1. Preheat the oven to 350°F. Lightly grease several cookie sheets and line with sheets of nonstick parchment paper. Melt the chocolate in a heatproof bowl set over a saucepan of simmering water. Alternatively, melt in the microwave according to the manufacturer's directions. Stir until smooth, then cool slightly.

2. Place the ground almonds in a food processor and add the sugar, almond extract, unsweetened cocoa, and one of the egg whites. Add the melted chocolate and a little of the other egg white, and blend to make a soft, smooth paste. Alternatively, place the ground almonds with the sugar, almond extract, and cocoa in a bowl, and make a well in the center. Add the melted chocolate with sufficient egg white, and gradually blend together to form a smooth, but not sticky, paste.

3. Shape the dough into small balls the size of large walnuts, and place them on the prepared cookie sheets. Flatten them slightly, then brush with a little water. Sprinkle a little confectioners' sugar over them, and cook in the preheated oven for 10–12 minutes until just firm.

4. Using a spatula, carefully lift the macaroons off the parchment paper and transfer to a wire rack to cool. These are best served immediately, but can be stored in an airtight container.

Traffic Lights

Makes 14

½ cup (1 stick) softened butter
⅓ cup superfine sugar
2 tbsp. light corn syrup
1 large egg, beaten
few drops vanilla extract
2¼ cups all-purpose flour, plus
  extra for dusting
1 tsp. baking powder

To decorate:

4 tbsp. strawberry jelly
4 tbsp. apricot jelly
4 tbsp. lime marmalade
confectioners' sugar,
  for dredging

1. Preheat the oven to 350°F. Grease two cookie sheets. Beat the butter, sugar, and syrup together until light and fluffy.

2. Gradually beat in the egg and vanilla extract. Sift the flour and baking powder into the bowl and stir into the mixture. Gather the mixture up with your hands and work it into a dough. Turn out onto a floured surface and knead gently until smooth. Wrap in plastic wrap and chill for 30 minutes.

3. Roll the pastry out to a thickness of ⅛ inch and cut into 28 oblongs measuring 1¼ x 3½ inches. Using the broad end of a piping tip or a cutter measuring ¾ inch wide, cut out three holes in each of 14 of the oblongs, remove the cut-out disks, and discard or re-roll to use as pastry trimmings. Place all the oblongs on the cookie sheets and bake for 8–10 minutes until golden. Transfer to a wire rack to cool.

4. Place 3 small teaspoonfuls of different colored jellies along the center of each rectangular cookie, starting with strawberry for red at the top, apricot for yellow in the middle, and lime marmalade for green at the bottom. Dust the cookies with the round holes with confectioners' sugar. Position these over the jellies on the rectangular cookies and press down so that the jellies show through.

Coconut & Almond Munchies

Makes 26–30

5 large egg whites
2¼ cups confectioners' sugar, plus extra to sprinkle
2 cups ground almonds
1¾ cups dried coconut
1 tbsp. grated lemon zest
4 oz. milk chocolate
4 oz. white chocolate

1. Preheat the oven to 300°F. Line several cookie sheets with rice paper. Place the egg whites in a clean, grease-free bowl, and beat until stiff and standing in peaks. Sift the confectioners' sugar, then carefully fold half the sugar into the beaten egg whites together with the ground almonds. Add the coconut, the remaining confectioners' sugar, and the lemon zest, and mix together to form a very sticky dough.

2. Place the dough in a piping bag and pipe the dough into walnut-size mounds onto the rice paper, then sprinkle with a little extra confectioners' sugar. Bake in the preheated oven for 20–25 minutes until set and golden on the outside. Remove from the oven and let cool slightly. Using a spatula, carefully transfer to a wire rack to cool.

3. Break the milk and white chocolate into pieces and place in two separate bowls. Melt both chocolates set over saucepans of gently simmering water. Alternatively, melt in the microwave according to the manufacturer's directions. Stir until smooth and free from lumps. Dip one edge of each munchie in the milk chocolate and let dry on nonstick parchment paper. When dry, dip the other side into the white chocolate. Let set, then serve as soon as possible.

Checkerboard Cookies

Makes 20

⅔ cup (1¼ sticks) butter
¾ cup confectioners' sugar
pinch salt
1¼ cups all-purpose flour
¼ cup unsweetened cocoa
1 medium egg white

1. Preheat the oven to 375°F. Lightly grease three or four cookie sheets. Place the butter and confectioners' sugar in a bowl, and cream together until light and fluffy.

2. Add the salt, then gradually add the flour, beating well after each addition. Mix well to form a firm dough. Cut the dough in half and knead the unsweetened cocoa into one half. Wrap both portions of dough separately in plastic wrap, and then let chill in the refrigerator for 2 hours.

3. Divide each piece of dough into three portions. Roll each portion of dough into a long roll, and arrange these rolls on top of each other to form a checkerboard design, sealing them with egg white. Wrap in plastic wrap and refrigerate for 1 hour.

4. Cut the dough into ¼-inch thick slices, place on the baking sheets, and bake for 10–15 minutes. Remove from the oven and let cool for a few minutes. Transfer to a wire rack and let cool before serving.

Rum & Chocolate Squares

Makes 14–16

½ cup (1 stick) butter
⅔ cup superfine sugar
pinch salt
2 large egg yolks
2 cups all-purpose flour
½ cup cornstarch
¼ tsp. baking powder
2 tbsp. unsweetened cocoa
1 tbsp. rum

1. Preheat the oven to 350°F. Lightly grease several cookie sheets. Cream the butter, sugar, and salt together in a large bowl until light and fluffy. Add the egg yolks and beat well until smooth.

2. Sift together 1½ cups of the flour, the cornstarch, and the baking powder, and add to the mixture. Mix well with a wooden spoon until a smooth and soft dough is formed.

3. Halve the dough and knead the unsweetened cocoa into one half and the rum and the remaining flour into the other half. Place the two batters in two separate bowls, cover with plastic wrap, and chill in the refrigerator for 1 hour.

4. Roll out both pieces of dough separately on a well-floured surface into two thin rectangles. Place one on top of the other, cut out squares, and place on the prepared baking sheets.

5. Bake in the preheated oven, half with the chocolate uppermost and the other half rum-side up, for 10–12 minutes until firm. Remove from the oven and let cool slightly. Using a spatula, transfer to a wire rack and let cool, then serve.

Chocolate Whirls

Makes 20

½ cup (4 oz.) soft margarine
6 tbsp. unsalted butter, softened
¾ cup confectioners' sugar, sifted
3 oz. semisweet dark chocolate,
  melted and cooled
2 tbsp. sifted cornstarch
1 cup all-purpose flour
1 cup self-rising flour

For the buttercream:
½ cup (1 stick)
  unsalted butter,
  softened
½ tsp. vanilla extract
2 cups sifted
  confectioners' sugar

1. Preheat the oven to 350°F. Lightly grease two large baking sheets. Cream the margarine, butter and confectioners' sugar together in a large bowl until the batter is light and fluffy.

2. Stir the chocolate until smooth, then beat into the creamed batter. Stir in the cornstarch. Sift the flours together, then gradually add to the creamed batter, a little at a time, beating well after each addition. Beat until the consistency is smooth and stiff enough for piping.

3. Put the batter in a decorating bag fitted with a large star tip, and pipe 40 small whirls onto the baking sheets.

4. Bake the whirls in the preheated oven for 12–15 minutes until firm to the touch. Remove from the oven and let cool for about 2 minutes. Using a spatula, transfer the whirls to wire racks and let cool.

5. Meanwhile, make the butter cream. Cream the butter with the vanilla extract until soft. Gradually beat in the confectioners' sugar and add a little cooled boiled water, if necessary, to give a smooth consistency.

6. When the chocolate whirls are completely cooled, pipe or spread on the prepared butter cream, sandwich together, and serve.

Pumpkin Cookies with Brown Butter Glaze

Makes 48

½ cup (1 stick) softened butter
1¼ cups all-purpose flour
¾ cup lightly packed light brown sugar
1⅓ cups canned pumpkin or cooked pumpkin
1 large egg, beaten
2 tsp. ground cinnamon
2½ tsp. vanilla extract
½ tsp. baking powder
½ tsp. baking soda
½ tsp. freshly grated nutmeg
½ cup whole-wheat flour
¾ cup coarsely chopped pecans
½ cup raisins
4 tbsp. unsalted butter
2 cups confectioners' sugar
2 tbsp. milk

1. Preheat the oven to 375°F. Lightly grease a baking sheet, and set aside.

2. Using an electric mixer, beat the butter until light and fluffy. Add the flour, sugar, pumpkin, and beaten egg, and beat with the mixer until well mixed.

3. Stir in the ground cinnamon and 1 teaspoon of the vanilla extract, then sift in the baking powder, baking soda, and grated nutmeg. Beat the mixture until well combined, scraping down the sides of the bowl.

4. Add the whole-wheat flour, chopped nuts, and raisins to the mixture, and fold in with a metal spoon or rubber spatula until mixed thoroughly. Place teaspoonfuls of the mixture about 2 inches apart on the baking sheet. Bake in the preheated oven for 10–12 minutes until the cookie edges are firm.

5. Remove the cookies from the oven and let cool on a wire rack. Meanwhile, melt the butter in a small saucepan over medium heat until pale and just turning golden brown.

6. Remove from the heat. Add the sugar, the remaining vanilla extract, and milk, stirring. Spread over the cooled cookies and serve.

Spiced Palmier Cookies

Makes 20

9 oz. prepared puff pastry, thawed if frozen
7 tbsp. superfine sugar
2 tbsp. confectioners' sugar
1 tsp. ground cinnamon
¼ tsp. ground ginger
¼ tsp. freshly grated nutmeg
1 lb. apples, coarsely chopped
¼ cup raisins
¼ cup dried cherries
zest of 1 orange
lightly whipped heavy cream, to serve

1. Preheat the oven to 400°F. Roll out the pastry on a lightly floured surface to form a 10 x 12-inch rectangle. Trim the edges. Sift 3 tablespoons of the superfine sugar, the confectioners' sugar, and spices into a bowl. Dust both sides of a pastry board with about a quarter of the mixture. With a long edge facing you, fold either side halfway toward the center. Dust with a third of the remaining sugar mixture. Fold each side again so that they almost meet, and dust again with about half the remaining sugar mixture. Fold the two sides together down the center of the pastry to give six layers altogether. Wrap the pastry in plastic wrap, and refrigerate for 1–2 hours until firm. Set aside the remaining spiced sugar.

2. Unwrap the chilled pastry and roll in the remaining sugar mixture to give a good coating. Cut into about 20 thin slices. Place cut-side down onto a baking sheet, and cook in the preheated oven for 10 minutes, then turn and cook for another 5–10 minutes, until golden and crisp. Remove from the oven, and let cool completely on a wire rack.

3. Combine the remaining superfine sugar and the rest of the ingredients in a saucepan. Cover and cook gently for 15 minutes until the apple is completely soft. Stir well and let cool. Serve with a spoonful of the apple sauce and a little of the whipped cream.

Peanut Butter Truffle Cookies

Makes 18

4 oz. semisweet dark chocolate
⅔ cup heavy cream
½ cup (1 stick) butter or margarine, softened
½ cup superfine sugar
½ cup crunchy or smooth peanut butter
4 tbsp. light corn syrup
1 tbsp. milk
2 cups all-purpose flour
½ tsp. baking soda

1. Preheat the oven to 350°F. Make the chocolate filling by breaking the chocolate into small pieces and placing in a heatproof bowl.

2. Put the heavy cream into a saucepan, and heat to boiling point. Immediately pour over the chocolate. Let stand for 1–2 minutes, then stir until smooth. Set aside to cool until firm enough to scoop. Do not refrigerate.

3. Lightly grease a baking sheet. Cream together the butter or margarine and the sugar until light and fluffy. Blend in the peanut butter, followed by the light corn syrup and milk.

4. Sift together the flour and baking soda. Add to the peanut butter mixture, mix well, and knead until smooth. Flatten 1–2 tablespoons of the cookie mixture on a pastry board. Put a spoonful of the chocolate mixture into the center of the cookie dough, then fold the dough around the chocolate to enclose completely.

5. Put the balls onto the baking sheet, and flatten slightly. Bake in the preheated oven for 10–12 minutes until golden. Remove from the oven and transfer to a wire rack to cool completely, then serve.

Chocolate & Ginger Florentines

Makes 14–16

3 tbsp. butter
5 tbsp. heavy cream
¼ cup superfine sugar
½ cup chopped almonds
½ cup slivered almonds
1½ tbsp. chopped candied ginger
¼ cup all-purpose flour
pinch salt
5 oz. semisweet dark chocolate

1. Preheat the oven to 350°F. Lightly grease several baking sheets. Melt the butter, cream, and sugar together in a saucepan, and bring slowly to a boil. Remove from the heat, and stir in the almonds and the candied ginger.

2. Let cool slightly, then mix in the flour and the salt. Blend together, then place heaping teaspoons of the batter on the baking sheets. Make sure they are spaced well apart, as they expand during cooking. Flatten them slightly with the back of a wet spoon.

3. Bake in the preheated oven for 10–12 minutes until just brown at the edges. Let cool slightly. Using a spatula, carefully transfer the Florentines to a wire rack and let cool.

4. Melt the chocolate in a heatproof bowl set over a saucepan of gently simmering water. Alternatively, melt the chocolate in the microwave, according to the manufacturer's directions, until just liquid and smooth. Spread thickly over one side of the Florentines, then mark wavy lines through the chocolate using a fork, and leave until firm.

Cherry Garlands

Makes 30

1 cup all-purpose flour
pinch salt
5 tbsp. butter, softened
¼ cup superfine sugar
1 large egg yolk
½ tsp. almond extract

To decorate:

12 candied cherries
1 egg white, lightly beaten
superfine sugar, for
  sprinkling

1. Preheat the oven to 375°F and grease two
   cookie sheets. Sift the flour and salt into a
   bowl or a food processor, add the butter,
   and rub in with your fingertips, or
   process until the mixture resembles fine
   crumbs. Stir in the sugar.

2. In another bowl, beat the egg yolk with
   the almond extract and add to the flour
   mixture. Stir to make a soft dough, then
   knead lightly. Roll the dough into pea-size balls
   and arrange 8 balls in a ring on a cookie sheet,
   pressing them together lightly.

3. Continue making rings until all the dough is used up.
   Cut each candied cherry into eight tiny wedges and
   place three on each cookie between the balls.

4. Bake for 14 minutes until golden, remove the cookies
   from the oven, and brush with beaten egg white.
   Sprinkle the tops lightly with superfine sugar, and
   return to the oven for 2 minutes until a sparkly glaze
   has formed. Let stand on the cookie sheets for 2
   minutes, then cool completely on a wire rack.

Lemon & Ginger Cookie-Cakes

Makes 15

¾ cup (1½ sticks) butter or margarine
3 cups all-purpose flour
2 tsp. baking powder
½ tsp. ground ginger
pinch salt
finely grated zest of 1 lemon
1 cup golden brown sugar
⅔ cup golden raisins
½ cup chopped candied peel
2 tbsp. finely chopped stem ginger
1 large egg
juice of 1 lemon

1. Preheat the oven to 425°F. Cut the butter or margarine into small pieces and place in a large bowl. Sift the flour, baking powder, ginger, and salt together, and add to the butter, along with the lemon zest.

2. Using your fingertips, rub the butter into the flour-and-spice mixture until it resembles coarse bread crumbs. Stir in the sugar, golden raisins, chopped candied peel, and stem ginger.

3. Add the egg and lemon juice to the mixture, then, using a round-bladed knife, stir well to mix. (The mixture should be quite stiff and just holding together.)

4. Place heaping tablespoons of the mixture onto a lightly greased baking tray, making sure that the dollops of mixture are well apart. Using a fork, roughen the edges of the buns and bake in the preheated oven for 12–15 minutes.

5. Leave the cookie-cakes to cool for 5 minutes before transferring to a wire rack. Let stand until cooled, then serve. Otherwise, store the cookie-cakes in an airtight container and eat within 3–5 days.

Bar
Cookies

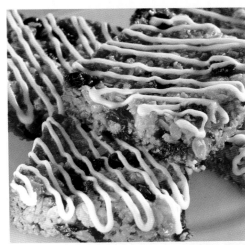

Fudgy Chocolate Bars

Makes 14

⅔ cup candied cherries
1 tbsp. shelled hazelnuts
5 oz. semisweet dark chocolate
⅔ cup (1¼ sticks) unsalted butter
¼ tsp. salt
1 cup Graham crackers, chopped into ¼-in. pieces
1 tbsp. confectioners' sugar, sifted (optional)

1. Preheat the oven to 350°F. Lightly grease a 7-inch square pan, and line the bottom with nonstick parchment paper. Rinse the candied cherries thoroughly, dry well on paper towels, and set aside.

2. Place the nuts on a baking pan and roast in the preheated oven for 10 minutes, or until light golden brown. Let cool slightly, then chop coarsely and set aside.

3. Break the chocolate into small pieces, and place with the butter and salt into the top of a double boiler or in a bowl set over a saucepan of gently simmering water. Heat gently, stirring, until melted and smooth. Alternatively, melt the chocolate in the microwave according to the manufacturer's directions.

4. Cut the cherries in half. Add to the chocolate mixture, along with the Graham crackers and nuts, and stir well. Spoon the batter into the prepared pan and level the top.

5. Chill in the refrigerator for 30 minutes, remove from the pan, discard the parchment paper, and cut into 14 bars. Cover lightly, return to the refrigerator, and keep chilled until ready to serve. To serve, lightly sprinkle the bars with sifted confectioners' sugar, if desired. Cover with plastic wrap and store in the refrigerator.

Classic Chewy Oat Bars

Makes 12

¾ cup (1½ sticks) butter, plus extra for greasing
⅔ cup turbinado (raw) sugar
2 tbsp. light corn syrup
scant 2 cups rolled oats
few drops vanilla extract

1. Preheat the oven to 325°F. Butter an 8-inch square baking pan.

2. Place the butter, sugar, and corn syrup in a saucepan and heat gently until the butter has melted and every grain of sugar has dissolved.

3. Remove from the heat and stir in the oats and vanilla extract. Stir well and then spoon the mixture into the prepared pan.

4. Smooth level with the back of a large spoon. Bake in the center of the preheated oven for 30–40 minutes until golden. Let stand to cool in the pan for 10 minutes, then mark into fingers and let stand in the pan until completely cold. When cold, cut into fingers with a sharp knife.

Fig & Chocolate Bars

Makes 12

½ cup (1 stick) butter
1¼ cups all-purpose flour
¼ cup firmly packed light brown sugar
1⅓ cups halved dried figs
juice of ½ a large lemon
1 tsp. ground cinnamon
4 oz. semisweet dark chocolate

1. Preheat the oven to 350°F. Lightly grease a 7-inch square cake pan. Place the butter and the flour in a large bowl and, using your fingertips, rub the butter into the flour until it resembles fine bread crumbs.

2. Stir in the sugar, then, using your hand, bring the batter together to form a dough. Knead until smooth, then press the dough into the prepared pan. Lightly prick the bottom with a fork, and bake in the preheated oven for 20–30 minutes until golden. Remove from the oven and let the shortbread cool in the pan until completely cooled.

3. Meanwhile, place the dried figs, lemon juice, ½ cup water, and the ground cinnamon in a saucepan, and bring to a boil. Cover, and simmer for 20 minutes, or until soft, stirring occasionally during cooking. Cool slightly, then puree in a food processor until smooth. Cool, then spread over the cooked shortbread.

4. Melt the chocolate in a heatproof bowl set over a saucepan of simmering water. Alternatively, melt the chocolate in the microwave according to the manufacturer's directions. Stir until smooth, then spread over the top of the fig filling. Leave to become firm, then cut into 12 bars and serve.

Chocolate-Covered Chewy Oat Bars

Makes 24

1¾ cups all-purpose flour
1¼ cups rolled oats
1 cup firmly packed light brown sugar
1 tsp. baking soda
pinch salt
⅔ cup (1¼ sticks) butter
2 tbsp. corn syrup
9 oz. semisweet dark chocolate
5 tbsp. heavy cream

1. Preheat the oven to 350°F. Lightly grease a 9 x 13-inch jelly-roll pan, and line with nonstick parchment paper. Place the flour, rolled oats, light brown sugar, baking soda, and salt into a bowl, and stir together well.

2. Melt the butter and corn syrup together in a heavy saucepan and stir until smooth, then add to the oat mixture and mix together thoroughly. Spoon the batter into the prepared pan, and press down firmly.

3. Bake in the preheated oven for 15–20 minutes until golden. Remove from the oven and let cool in the pan. Once cool, remove from the pan. Discard the parchment paper.

4. Melt the chocolate in a heatproof bowl set over a saucepan of gently simmering water. Alternatively, melt the chocolate in the microwave according to the manufacturer's directions. Once the chocolate has melted, quickly beat in the cream, then pour over the oat base. Mark patterns over the chocolate with a fork when almost set.

5. Chill in the refrigerator for at least 30 minutes before cutting into bars. When the chocolate has set, serve. Store in an airtight container for a few days.

Nanaimo Bars

Makes 15

6 tbsp. unsalted butter
4 oz. semisweet dark chocolate, coarsely chopped
1 cup Graham cracker crumbs
¾ cup dried coconut
½ cup chopped mixed nuts

For the filling:
1 large egg yolk
1 tbsp. milk
6 tbsp. unsalted butter, softened
1 tsp. vanilla extract
1¼ cups confectioners' sugar

For the topping:
4 oz. semisweet dark chocolate, coarsely chopped
2 tsp. sunflower oil

1. Grease and line a 1 x 7 x 11-inch cake pan with nonstick parchment paper. Place the butter and chocolate in a small, heatproof bowl set over a saucepan of almost-boiling water until melted, stirring occasionally. Stir in the crumbs, coconut, and nuts into the chocolate mixture and mix well. Spoon into the prepared pan and press down firmly. Chill in the refrigerator for 20 minutes.

2. For the filling, place the egg yolk and milk in a bowl set over a saucepan of almost-boiling water. Make sure the bowl does not touch the water. Beat for 2–3 minutes. Add the butter and vanilla extract and continue beating until fluffy. Gradually beat in the confectioners' sugar. Spread over the chilled mixture, smoothing with the back of a spoon, and chill in the refrigerator for an additional 30 minutes.

3. For the topping, place the chocolate and corn oil in a heatproof bowl set over a saucepan of almost-boiling water. Melt, stirring occasionally, until smooth. Let cool slightly, then pour over the filling and tilt the pan so that the chocolate spreads evenly. Chill in the refrigerator for about 5 minutes until the chocolate topping is just set but not too hard, then mark into 15 bars. Chill again for 2 hours, then cut into slices and serve.

Marbled Toffee Shortbread

Makes 12

¾ cup (1½ sticks) butter
½ cup superfine sugar
2 cups all-purpose flour
¼ cup unsweetened cocoa

For the toffee filling:

4 tbsp. butter
¼ cup firmly packed golden brown sugar
14 oz. canned condensed milk

For the chocolate topping:

3 oz. semisweet dark chocolate
3 oz. milk chocolate
3 oz. white chocolate

1. Preheat the oven to 350°F. Grease and line an 8-inch square cake pan with nonstick parchment paper. Cream the butter and sugar together until light and fluffy, then sift in the flour and unsweetened cocoa. Mix together to form a soft dough. Press into the bottom of the prepared pan. Prick all over with a fork, then bake in the preheated oven for 25 minutes. Let cool.

2. To make the toffee filling, gently heat the butter, sugar, and condensed milk together until the sugar has dissolved. Bring to a boil, then simmer for 5 minutes, stirring continuously. Leave for 1 minute, then spread over the shortbread and let cool.

3. For the topping, place the different chocolates in separate heatproof bowls and melt one at a time, set over a saucepan of almost-boiling water. Drop spoonfuls of each on top of the toffee and tilt the pan to cover evenly. Swirl with a knife for a marbled effect.

4. Let the chocolate cool. When just set, mark into fingers using a sharp knife. Leave for at least 1 hour to harden before cutting into fingers.

Luxury Rocky Road Bars

Makes 12

14 pink and white marshmallows
½ cup dried mixed fruit
3 tbsp. chopped candied orange peel
3 tbsp. quartered candied cherries
¼ cup chopped walnuts
1 tbsp. brandy
2¼ cups Graham cracker crumbs
8 oz. semisweet dark chocolate
½ cup (1 stick) unsalted butter
1 tbsp. confectioners' sugar, for dusting (optional)

1. Lightly grease and line the bottom of a 7-inch pan with nonstick parchment paper. Using greased kitchen scissors, snip each marshmallow into four or five pieces over a bowl. Add the dried mixed fruit, orange peel, cherries, and walnuts to the bowl. Sprinkle with the brandy and stir together. Add the crumbs and stir until mixed.

2. Break the chocolate into small pieces and put in a heatproof bowl with the butter, set over a saucepan of almost-boiling water. Stir occasionally until melted, then remove from the heat. Pour the chocolate over the dry ingredients and mix well. Spoon into the prepared pan, pressing down firmly.

3. Chill in the refrigerator for 15 minutes, then mark into 12 fingers using a sharp knife. Chill in the refrigerator for an additional hour, or until set. Turn out of the pan, remove the lining paper, and cut into fingers. Dust with confectioners' sugar before serving.

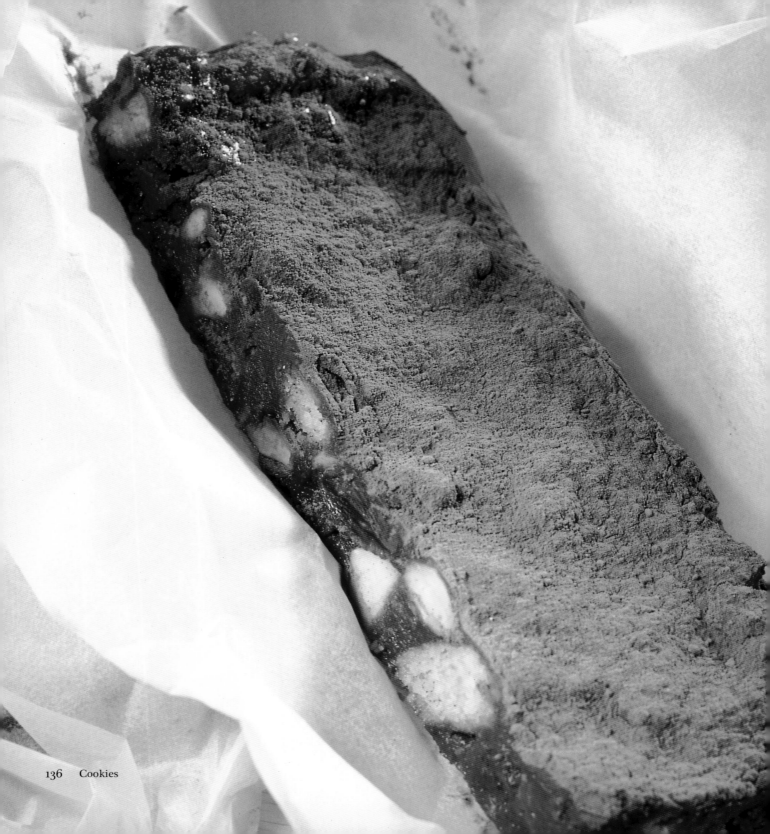

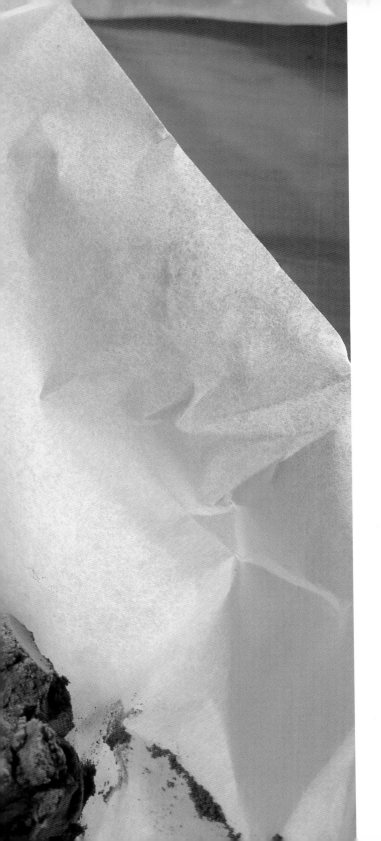

Chocolate Cookie Bars

Makes 20

⅓ cup golden raisins
3–4 tbsp. brandy (optional)
3½ oz. semisweet dark chocolate
½ cup (1 stick) unsalted butter
2 tbsp. light corn syrup
⅔ cup heavy cream
6 Graham crackers, coarsely crushed
½ cup toasted and coarsely chopped shelled pistachio nuts
½ cup toasted and coarsely chopped blanched almonds
¼ cup coarsely chopped candied cherries
grated zest of 1 orange
unsweetened cocoa, sifted

1. Lightly grease an 8-inch square pan and line with plastic wrap. Place the golden raisins into a small bowl, and pour over the brandy, if using. Let soak for 20–30 minutes.

2. Meanwhile, break the chocolate into small pieces and put into a heatproof bowl. Place the bowl over a saucepan of simmering water, making sure that the bottom of the bowl does not touch the water. Leave the chocolate until melted, stirring occasionally. Remove from the heat.

3. Add the butter, light corn syrup, and heavy cream to a small saucepan, and heat until the butter has melted.

4. Remove the saucepan from the heat, and add the melted chocolate, cookies, nuts, cherries, orange zest, golden raisins, and the brandy marinade, if using. Mix thoroughly and pour into the prepared pan. Smooth the top and chill in the refrigerator for at least 4 hours until firm.

5. Turn out the cake and remove the plastic wrap. Dust liberally with the unsweetened cocoa, then cut into bars to serve. Store lightly covered in the refrigerator.

Miracle Bars

Makes 12

7 tbsp. butter, melted, plus 1–2 tsp. extra for greasing
1½ cups Graham cracker crumbs
¼ cup chocolate chips
1 cup shredded coconut
1 cup chopped mixed nuts
16 oz. canned sweetened condensed milk

1. Preheat the oven to 350°F. Butter a 9-inch square pan and line with a layer of nonstick parchment paper.

2. Pour the butter into the prepared pan, and sprinkle the Graham cracker crumbs over in an even layer.

3. Add the chocolate chips, coconut, and nuts in even layers, and drizzle over the condensed milk.

4. Transfer the pan to the preheated oven, and bake for 30 minutes until golden brown. Let cool in the pan, then cut into 12 squares, and serve.

Pecan Caramel Millionaire's Shortbread

Makes 20

½ cup (1 stick) softened butter
2 tbsp. smooth peanut butter
6 tbsp. superfine sugar
½ cup cornstarch
1½ cups all-purpose flour

For the topping:

scant 1 cup superfine sugar
½ cup (1 stick) butter
2 tbsp. light corn syrup
3 tbsp. liquid glucose
6 tbsp. water
16 oz. canned sweetened condensed milk
1½ cups coarsely chopped pecans
3 oz. semisweet dark chocolate
1 tbsp. butter

1. Preheat the oven to 350°F. Lightly grease and line a 7 x 11-inch pan with wax paper or parchment paper. Cream together the butter, peanut butter, and sugar until light. Sift in the cornstarch and flour together, and mix in to make a smooth dough. Press the mixture into the prepared pan, and prick all over with a fork. Bake in the preheated oven for 20 minutes until just golden. Remove from the oven.

2. Meanwhile, for the topping, combine the sugar, butter, light corn syrup, glucose, water, and milk in a heavy saucepan. Stir continuously over low heat, without boiling, until the sugar has dissolved. Increase the heat, and boil, stirring continuously, for about 10 minutes until the mixture turns a caramel color. Remove the saucepan from the heat and add the pecans. Pour over the shortbread base immediately. Let cool, then refrigerate for at least 1 hour.

3. Break the chocolate into small pieces, put into a heatproof bowl, along with the butter, then place over a saucepan of barely simmering water, making sure that the bowl does not come into contact with the water. Leave until melted, then stir together well. Remove the shortbread from the refrigerator and pour the chocolate evenly over the top, spreading thinly to cover. Let set, cut into squares, and serve.

Fruit & Nut Chewy Oat Bars

Makes 12

6 tbsp. butter or margarine
½ cup light brown sugar
3 tbsp. corn syrup
½ cup raisins
½ cup coarsely chopped walnuts
scant 1 cup rolled oats
5 tbsp. confectioners' sugar
1–1½ tbsp. lemon juice

1. Preheat the oven to 350°F. Lightly grease a 9-inch square cake pan.

2. Melt the butter or margarine with the sugar and syrup in a small saucepan over low heat. Remove from the heat.

3. Stir the raisins, walnuts, and oats into the syrup mixture, and mix together. Spoon the oat mixture evenly into the prepared pan and press down firmly. Transfer to the preheated oven, and bake for 20–25 minutes. Remove from the oven and let cool in the pan. Cut into bars while still warm.

4. Sift the confectioners' sugar into a small bowl, then gradually beat in the lemon juice, a little at a time, to form a thin icing. Place into a decorating bag fitted with a writing tip, then pipe thin lines over the oat bars. Let cool, then serve.

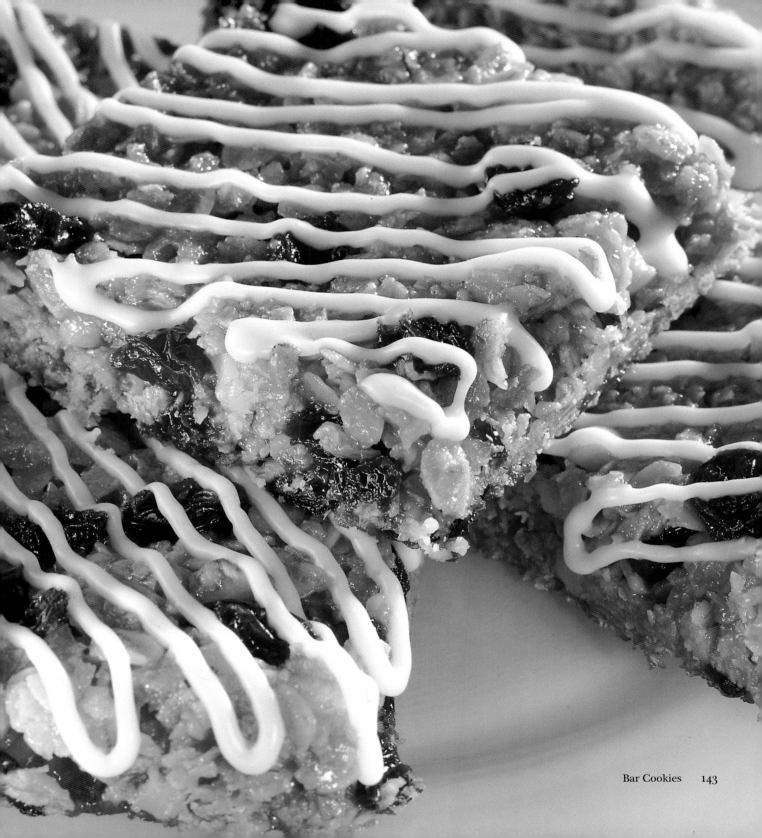

Index